Equity, Equality, and Empathy

Equity, Equality, and Empathy

What Principals Can Do for the Well-Being of the Learning Community

Richard D. Sorenson

ROWMAN & LITTLEFIELD
Lanham • Boulder • New York • London

Published by Rowman & Littlefield
An imprint of The Rowman & Littlefield Publishing Group, Inc.
4501 Forbes Boulevard, Suite 200, Lanham, Maryland 20706
www.rowman.com

86-90 Paul Street, London EC2A 4NE, United Kingdom

Copyright © 2022 by Richard D. Sorenson

All rights reserved. No part of this book may be reproduced in any form or by any electronic or mechanical means, including information storage and retrieval systems, without written permission from the publisher, except by a reviewer who may quote passages in a review.

British Library Cataloguing in Publication Information Available

Library of Congress Cataloging-in-Publication Data

Names: Sorenson, Richard D., author.
Title: Equity, equality, and empathy : what principals can do for the well-being of the learning community / Richard D. Sorenson.
Description: Lanham, Maryland : Rowman & Littlefield, [2022] | Includes bibliographical references and index. | Summary: "Equity, Equality, and Empathy is written for principals to gain expertise upon the successful incorporation of seven actions related to the advancement of equity, equality, and empathy by means of developing a well-being program which nurtures a positive campus climate and culture through research-based social and emotional learning processes"—Provided by publisher.
Identifiers: LCCN 2022015842 (print) | LCCN 2022015843 (ebook) | ISBN 9781475866063 (Cloth : acid-free paper) | ISBN 9781475866070 (Paperback : acid-free paper) | ISBN 9781475866087 (epub)
Subjects: LCSH: School principals—In-service training—United States. | Educational leadership—United States. | Affective education—United States.
Classification: LCC LB1738.5 .S57 2022 (print) | LCC LB1738.5 (ebook) | DDC 371.2/012–dc23/eng/20220701
LC record available at https://lccn.loc.gov/2022015842
LC ebook record available at https://lccn.loc.gov/2022015843

Dedicated to Lloyd Goldsmith.
Great friend, former administrative colleague, fellow emeriti professor, and longtime writing partner. Our parallel careers and educational experiences brought much joy to work and life!
Ah, the memories, mi amigo!

Contents

Acknowledgments	ix
Introduction: Principal Actions	xi
Chapter 1: Principal Action #1: Find a Cure	1
Chapter 2: Principal Action #2: Develop a Successful Well-Being Program	19
Chapter 3: Principal Action #3: Embrace Social and Emotional Learning	35
Chapter 4: Principal Action #4: Appreciate Social and Emotional Learning	55
Chapter 5: Principal Action #5: Distinguish Between Equity and Equality	73
Chapter 6: Principal Action #6: Ensure Empathy Is a Campus and Cultural Norm	95
Chapter 7: Principal Action #7: Strengthen Your Own Personal Leadership Skills with the Social and Emotional Learning Instrument (A Principal Protocol)	109
Note	113
References	115
Index	125
About the Author	131

Acknowledgments

Xavier Barrera (1945–2020). You made my administrative career so much more fulfilling with your great humor, contagious laughter, exceptional mentoring, seasoned advice, and brotherly love. I miss you, my friend.

A debt of gratitude to and appreciation for Tom Koerner, vice president/senior editor, education division of Rowman & Littlefield, Publishers Inc. Thank you, Tom, for the writing opportunities.

Donna, your loving encouragement has always made me a better man, school administrator, scholar, and writer! Thank you, sweetheart, for always being there. Thank you for all of the numerous chapter readings and edits. You cause me to smile, and you make my life complete!

FRONT COVER IMAGE

The front cover image—showcasing a compass—was purposefully selected as it correlates with the theme of the text: Principals, much like a compass, must ensure that any academic journey (program, activity, or initiative) is prudent in direction, and equitable and equal by all standards of measurement. Such educational and leadership passages must always be laser-focused and follow an empathetic course in terms of actions and behaviors, cautiously calibrated and point-to-point directed—all as a means of best aiming for, guiding, and reaching the social and emotional well-being of all students, faculty and staff, parents, community members, and principals, too!

Introduction
Principal Actions

I have promises to keep, and miles to go before I sleep
The school is lovely, but can be dark and deep,
But I have promises to keep, and miles to go before I sleep.

(Adapted from the Robert Frost poem "Stopping by Woods on a Snowy Evening," 1923/1969)

The introduction subtitle, "Principal Actions," is one with a double meaning. The term *principal* is more than a title for a school leader. The word also correlates with another meaning—that of "main, major, primary, or key." Therefore, the title of the introduction is bi-corollary or bi-consequential: *Principal* is the main, major, primary, or key reason appropriate and effective actions can occur at a school. The second word, *actions*—from a principal's perspective—must always be regarded as measures, activities, behaviors, or procedures which are "fundamental, foremost, or critically important."

The second segment of the introduction comes from the Robert Frost poem "Stopping by Woods on a Snowy Evening" (1923/1969), and gives reference to the work conducted by exceptional principals. These school leaders always have promises to keep and miles to go before they sleep. Exceptional principals are dedicated leaders and tireless workers—always thinking, always helping, and always committing to those promises they have made to themselves and to others to best benefit the well-being of all members of a learning community.

These exceptional principals are selfless, devoted to the students they serve, and organized and prepared. They embrace the leadership role; anticipate, adjust, learn, recognize, understand, and embrace diversity; meet, greet, and engage in good humor; and always understand the powers and problems that come with school leadership. These principals have miles to go before they sleep, and certainly, many promises to keep!

Effective principal actions correlate with more than principal success. Principal actions—particularly those that are wise, transparent, student-centered, academically focused, research-based, and best-practice–oriented—are essential to the academic success of all students. Other principal actions based on strong moral and ethical standards, empathy, equity, and equality lead to the success of the entire learning community, most notably, students and their social and emotional well-being. When students achieve and succeed, all members of the learning community do—including the principal.

Therefore, principal actions must be honest, deliberate, collaborative, facilitative, and always in the best interest of students. Principal actions must be empathetic, always ensuring student equity and equality. No wonder, the very best principals agree, figuratively and often literally, that they have many promises to keep and definitely many miles to go before they sleep!

Exceptional principals recognize there are aspects of schooling that can be dark and deep; thus, they focus on and address the well-being of students, teachers, parents, and community, and guide the training of social and emotional learning (SEL). These school leaders teach and coach the positive impact of intellectual and emotional wellness, along with what it means to be individuals of equity, equality, and empathy.

Therefore, *Equity, Equality, and Empathy: What Principals Can Do for the Well-Being of the Learning Community* is all about focusing on leadership actions related to fairness, justness, and justice, along with parity, uniformity, and a total and equal opportunity for all, as well as an understanding, compassion, and responsiveness for the well-being of every member of a learning community. These considerations are the underlying basis for the book.

- Chapter 1, "Principal Action #1: Find a Cure," presents an examination of the differences between wellness and well-being, noting that well-being is all about the positive emotions and moods exuded within and across a learning community. Well-being is all about pleasure, joyfulness, and satisfaction in place of negative emotions and those prevailing winds of dismay, inequity, and inequality which can push through a school, leaving behind an affliction that must be empathetically addressed and cured. Identified within the chapter are 10 strategies for school principals to incorporate which are essential for the well-being of a learning community.
- Chapter 2, "Principal Action #2: Develop a Successful Well-Being Program," explores how principals must take responsibility for fostering the well-being of all members of the learning community by advancing

advocacy, teaming, building relationships, meeting, discussing, problem-solving, and sharing and strengthening all aspects of teaching, leading, and learning. Each action positively impacts student emotional well-being, equity and equality, performance, and achievement.

- Chapter 3, "Principal Action #3: Embrace Social and Emotional Learning," discloses a seven-step process by which principals help students, teachers, and parents welcome, appreciate, and adopt goals and expectations related to implementing a strong SEL program based on equity, equality, and empathy.
- Chapter 4, "Principal Action #4: Appreciate Social and Emotional Learning," reveals seven benefits of incorporating SEL into a school's curriculum and instructional process. Additionally, seven challenges associated with SEL implementation are examined with guidance as to how said challenges can be overcome via strong and effective principal leadership.
- Chapter 5, "Principal Action #5: Distinguish Between Equity and Equality," prompts principals to understand that far too many social injustices plague the nation and school systems and how such are related to (in)equity and (in)equality. Revealed are TOP-10 Steps to Quality Leadership effective in guiding campus leaders when working with others in overcoming biases, prejudices, and discriminatory actions and practices. Moreover, 14 school-oriented processes to eradicating racism in schools and schooling are identified and addressed, as well as six critical standards principals must commit to as a means of best ensuring equity and equality throughout a learning community.
- Chapter 6, "Principal Action #6: Ensure Empathy Is a Campus and Cultural Norm," promotes seven elements of empathy and how such are critical tools for effective school leadership. Additionally, seven habits of highly empathetic principals are explored along with five steps to a principal establishing and maintaining a learning community climate and culture of empathy.
- Chapter 7, "Principal Action #7: Strengthen Your Own Personal Leadership Skills with the Social and Emotional Learning Instrument (A Principal Protocol)" investigates, by means of a critical skills inventory, how principals or prospective principals personally react to SEL, equity and equality, and empathetic leadership. The survey instrument permits an individual to honestly reflect upon how the mastery of key leadership skills is essential to developing a learning community based on hope, well-being, empathy, equity, and equality.

Special features of the book include the following:

- Vignettes/scenarios applicable to principal leadership
- Related textboxes
- Pause and consider questions
- Leadership protocol and self-reflective learning instrument
- Discussion questions
- Case study applications and questions
- References

Moreover, the book is suitable for self and group book studies, workshops, education courses, and professional development sessions. The target audience is current and prospective K–12 administrators, university principal preparation programs, as well as teachers and student teachers.

Conclusively, *Equity, Equality, and Empathy: What Principals Can Do for the Well-Being of the Learning Community* is not designed to be an exhaustive study of SEL and well-being, and of equity, equality, empathy, racism, and social justice. Nor is the book intended to merely provide a basic understanding of these timely topics.

Instead, the contents provide the essential information and associated actions decisive in providing principals with crucial competencies, critical proficiencies, and vital skills to initiate appropriate social, emotional, and racial and radical changes in education. Therefore, as a principal leader or potential leader, seize the day, make a valiant and valuable leadership difference, and enjoy the read!

Chapter 1

Principal Action #1
Find a Cure

SCHOOLS TODAY: IS WELLNESS OR WELL-BEING THE ANTIDOTE?

"I'm a therapist, and this is why neglecting our student's mental health could be lethal, today!"—Sheila Robinson-Kiss (2020)

WHAT IS WELLNESS? WHAT IS WELL-BEING? WHICH IS THE BETTER APPLICATION AND A GREATER ANTIDOTE FOR SCHOOLS?

During a Black Lives Matter protest, in the midst of the ever-increasing threat of spreading the COVID-19 virus, and ignited by a ticking time bomb that exploded as a result of the appalling 2020 murder of Houston native and Minneapolis resident George Floyd, therapist Sheila Robinson-Kiss revealed an absolute every principal must know and every teacher must understand: "Health maintenance must be the personal fire hydrant we use to extinguish the flames of stress, fatigue, and anxiety that are roaring today. Self-care is no longer an option" (Robinson-Kiss, 2020).

Self-care has long been the irresponsible remedy for students in schools who are suffering from the plague of social-emotional abandonment. Self-care has seldom worked, especially when tending to an open wound that simply won't heal without the aid of a trauma unit. This unit, a trauma center called school, requires specially trained personnel to cure devalued individuals, mostly of color, long abandoned in teaching, leading, and learning environments.

Most troubling, far too many learning communities are grossly void of psychological, financial, social, and political treatments designed to bring a long-awaited antidote. The antidote? Principal Action #1: Find a Cure for a degrading illness affecting many students. The illness is a lack of wellness that is, at the very least, debilitating, and at the worst, life threatening, if not extinguishing.

Hard facts are often difficult to swallow, if not stomach. But tough times require resolute answers to the most difficult questions. Consider these four: What is wellness? What is well-being? Which is the greater antidote for learning communities? Which, as a matter of fact, is the better application in schools?

Wellness or Well-Being: A Critical Examination

Wellness is related to the health and care of the physical body as well as the mental and emotional state of the mind. Wellness emphasizes the prevention of illnesses and the prolonging of life with a conscious, oftentimes self-directed therapeutic application. Well-being, while similar in definition to wellness, is a better descriptor and relates to life satisfaction and genuine feelings extending across a spectrum spanning from depression to joyfulness.

Well-being is all about positive emotions and moods such as contentment, happiness, pleasure, joyfulness, and satisfaction, as well as the absence of negative emotions such as depression, anxiety, dejection, sadness, despair, and hopelessness. Principals must ask themselves and all members of the learning community if the students served are satisfied with their lives, fulfilled in their home and school settings, positively functioning, perceive their lives optimistically and constructively, and have overall good feelings about schooling.

Well-being, again often synonymous in discussion and literature with wellness, relates to positive psychology. Are students emotionally positive, actively engaged, developing positive relationships and social networks, finding purpose and meaning in both life and schooling, connected to a greater good, setting goals as a means of accomplishment, and generally satisfied in terms of actualizing capabilities? Studies indicate that students who are satisfied in life are interested in building and broadening their individual strengths and capabilities while avoiding, when humanly possible, the negative effects of life such as distress, suffering, anxiety, dejection, misery, trauma, depression, and unhappiness (Noble, McGrath, Wyatt, Carbines, & Robb, 2008).

The focus, therefore, of this chapter and text, from a principal action and leadership perspective, relates to the overarching theme of and focus on the well-being of students. Research has readily linked well-being to learning (Jones & Kahn, 2017; Kendziora & Yoder, 2016). The well-being of a student at school, as a cure, is reflected in attitude, satisfaction, engagement in learning, and positive social-emotional behaviors. Well-being in school is characterized by positive feelings and attitudes toward self and others, high levels of satisfaction, and optimism—all of which are correlated with actualized learning and academic achievement.

Yet, a problem exists. The issue at hand is an affliction that is ever-pervading throughout schools across the nation. What is the problem, issue, affliction, or depriving symptom, and what's a principal to do when pursuing and initiating Principal Action #1: Find a Cure?

WHAT IS THE EVER-PERVADING SYMPTOM, WEAKNESS, OR AFFLICTION, AND IS THERE A CURE?

Are students in schools today socially and emotionally well? Many would say no. If the affirmative is overwhelmed by the negative, what exactly is the problem and, just as important, what is the cure? Throughout this and subsequent chapters, more detailed explanations, with potential solutions, will shed further light on the preceding question.

The Affliction: A Condition Worthy of Treatment

Principals must acknowledge that student well-being is a critical concern in schools today. The positive development of students' social, emotional, behavioral, and academic advancement is at war with escalating rates of youth depression, suicide, self-harm, anti-social behaviors (violence and bullying, to name just two actions), racial inequities and inequalities, and drug and alcohol abuse and addiction. The problem, the affliction, is intensifying at an alarming rate. How can students learn, teachers instruct, and principals lead if disadvantages in student life are brought into schools and classrooms? One principal noted, "Simple question, difficult answer." True. But not an impossible solution!

For many decades, the prevailing winds have pushed an air of dismay throughout schools. Principals, teachers, district administrators, parents, community and business leaders, and even students have long recognized a drastic change—a change in student behaviors, actions, and conduct all negatively intensifying and affecting teaching, leading, and learning.

Programs have been developed, purchased, frequently funded by grant and foundation dollars, and implemented. Character education, wellness (albeit student physical health) initiatives, school-community reforms, values education, self-respect activities, supportive learning, student voice projects, and even cooperative learning have long been advanced. Have these programs worked? Yes and no. Still, the overall symptoms remain and while antidotes have been administered, the problem has grown worse. Why? One reason: School systems, district administrators, principals, and school personnel have all too often either ignored, or simply failed to model and promote, the well-being of students.

Attendance and Suspensions: The Effects of Disciplinary Issues and Actions on Student Well-Being

The well-being of students, notably students of color, and the effect on achievement readily relates to attendance, discipline reform, out-of-school suspension, in-school suspension, expulsion, and other school disciplinary issues (FutureEd, 2020; Steinberg & Lacoe, 2017). Consider the following research and recommended practices which aid in student well-being.

Recent research has suggested, what the very best principals have long perceived, that expulsions and suspensions of students for non-violent disciplinary conduct benefit neither the suspended students nor their peers and that the reduction of such disciplinary tools or tactics must be complemented by district-level policy reforms coupled with intensive school-level supports (that is, better and more rigorous counseling and therapeutic efforts, a greater counselor-student ratio, student success team, "push-in" classroom instruction, and after-school learning sessions).

How are these "well-being" principal actions, reforms, efforts, and methods to better help students and school personnel find a cure to overcoming the stigmatization of negative, if not often abusive, disciplinary techniques? First, principals and their faculty must create student success teams (core teachers, administrators, guidance counselors, and associated therapists) who will monitor, assist, and accelerate students, both academically and in terms of their positive well-being. Second, principals must engage team members in the development of learning community leaders who will collect and analyze data to enhance the learning and achievement of those students in crisis and thus needing serious support and multi-tiered interventions.

Third, "push-in" classroom instruction is required to work with students with organizational, study skills issues, and home and life impairments. Intensive, rigorous, if not exhaustive teaching strategies are required to aid these students in helping them to best relate to, accept, and understand the subject matter. Fourth, after-school learning sessions (more than tutorials) are required for not only academic considerations but for extra support—socially, emotionally, and behaviorally.

Finally, how and by what means? Behavioral interventions, disciplinary actions, and academic support and achievement must be tethered to student well-being. The research is clear and unflinching: Both in- and out-of-school suspensions and expulsions negatively impact not only student attendance but student achievement, positive teacher-student interactions, and on-campus well-being efforts and expands racial disparity (Steinberg & Lacoe, 2017). More specifically, principals and teams must model and promote emotional well-being.

MODEL AND PROMOTE EMOTIONAL WELL-BEING

Stress, anxiety, hypertension, and other medical issues complicate communities—especially those of color. More than half of all Black adults in the United States are affected by these medical conditions (Robinson-Kiss, 2020). Latinx adults over the age of 20 are twice as likely to suffer from diabetes (Centers for Disease Control and Prevention, 2019). Medical concerns negatively affect people and their emotions and, thus, their well-being.

Personnel Are Affected, Too!

Individuals who are stressed, anxiety-ridden, and suffering medically with few avenues for help are the same people who are emotionally drained. Often, these individuals have little hope. Sometimes they reach a point of simply making peace with trouble. Even principals and teachers suffer: 54% of principals experience great stress daily (Moore, 2018), and 93% of teachers report experiencing high stress levels (Smiley, 2020). Whether students or personnel, to whom can they turn for help? Politicians? Police? Clergy? Social workers? School counselors, or others?

Consider the following account and then contemplate the questions that ensue:

> "MAKING PEACE WITH TROUBLE!"
>
> Chanice Kobolowski, a teacher at North Brookglen School, spent all day Saturday with her children shopping for groceries and new winter coats for her three kids (ages 10, 7, and 4). It was a cold, drizzling December day—with Christmas quickly approaching. Chanice and her children were out of school for the holidays, and it was an opportunity to stock up for the big Christmas-day meal with the grandparents, and to get the kids some much needed winter wear.
>
> Miles, the late husband of Chanice, and the father of her three children, died unexpectedly of a heart attack the previous June. Miles Kobolowski, too, was an educator—a school administrator. Stress, anxiety, and an undetected heart

valve issue had culminated in his untimely passing. Life had been difficult during the six-months following his death. Yet, Chanice managed but not without her own levels of grief, high stress, anxiety, fear, and recurring thoughts of dread and doom.

Today, however, as Chanice Kobolowski drove home with laughter filling the car, she and the kids suddenly noticed smoke emitting from beneath the hood of their vehicle. Almost home, Chanice realized the needle of the car's temperature gauge was rocketing into the "red" danger zone. She continued driving, slowly, and soon pulled into the drive of their home. Chanice killed the engine and she and the kids jumped out of the car. Smoke bellowed from beneath the hood of the car. The engine huffed, clattered, and sizzled. Slowly, oozing from beneath the car was a thick oily black substance.

Neighbor Marcie Dalhgren-Frost walked across the street from her home and up the Kobolowski's drive. Marcie was a good friend and of all things, not only a car enthusiast but a well-trained mechanic and owner of Elite Automotive. Marcie popped the hood, stepped to the side of the smoldering heat and rising smoke, and observed. Then, she turned to Chanice and said: "You've blown your head gasket. Let's get it towed into the shop and I'll have my crew work on it come Monday."

Chanice asked: "How much, Marcie?" Marcie replied: "It'll be a pretty penny or two, but I'll see that we make you a good deal. I know times are tough." Chanice Kobolowski didn't know much about car repairs, but she suspected a repair price tag of at least $1000.00, probably more. Her heart sank as she was still paying for her husband's funeral expenses.

Her husband had life insurance on Chanice and the kids but none on himself. Chanice had recently sunk additional money from her limited savings into other home repair expenses—a new heating system, a broken water-line, and just last week, a new washing machine. Chanice Kobolowski bitterly groaned out loud: "Why can't things just work? Why can't stuff stop breaking on me?"

Neighbor Marcie gave Chanice a hug and held her tight. Chanice broke down and cried out: "How can I take heart when this world causes me so much despair and I have so much to overcome? I'm not certain I'll ever be able to make peace with all this trouble!"

If the responsibilities of leading and teaching at a school are not, at times, overwhelming enough, life outside of school, for many principals, teachers, and students, too, can be a tremendous burden. Even a tenet of major religions reminds us: "In this world you will have trouble" (Gopin, 1997).

Pause and Consider

Identified below are supportive mental and emotional health service options available to individuals such as Chanice Kobolowski. These well-being options will not only help Chanice and her family but others across a learning community (especially students) in overcoming a lack of supportive services when combined with self-neglect, self-care, and self-controlling emotional issues which often lead to the direst of circumstances, and sometimes, sadly, a death sentence. Principals must recognize, accept, and willingly share the following:

- *Take advantage of free therapy.* While most therapists charge upward of $200.00 per hour for consultation services, high-quality, transformational help is available on YouTube and other digital outlets. Google "YouTube Therapy" as a means of helping students, their families, and school personnel. For students and families who do not have Internet access or a digital means of accessing the site, provide a tablet or laptop, for example, with a Wi-Fi hotspot. Additionally, seek community therapy that is free of charge. There are therapists who provide pro bono services, especially to students.
- *Empty emotional stress and strain daily.* A toxic buildup of "stinking-thinking" emotions is a real phenomenon today. Can't afford or don't have time for a therapist? Do this and unload the heaviest of emotions: Pull up a chair and have a seat directly across from an empty chair. In the privacy of home, start talking out loud and unload all of those heavy burdens.
- *Engage an accountability friend.* Between two friends, like Chanice and Marcie, establish emotional well-being goals and keep track of progress made. Meet face-to-face or give one another a call at least once a week. Talking and accountability bring positive results. Now, respond to the following questions.
    1. Contemplate the three above noted and bulleted items. Which one might best aid Chanice Kobolowski in her quest to find emotional peace? Explain why.
    2. Consider a different approach to emotionally helping the well-being of Chanice Kobolowski. Identify and share your idea(s).
    3. School personnel, including principals, are often in definite need of emotional help. What mental health assistance is available on your campus to aid members of a learning community? Identify such well-being resources.
    4. Unfortunately, too many members of a learning community, especially students, are often lost in the system, swept away—often unconsciously—by the tides of busyness, avoidance, or neglect. Students, and personnel, too, can all too frequently feel emotionally and psychologically helpless if not hopeless, devalued, and degraded to a breaking point. In your school, how is the well-being of others supported?

RECOGNIZE THE GREAT NEED FOR HOPE AND OPTIMISM: A PRINCIPAL ACTION LEADING TO A CURE

The year 2020 featured a financial crisis, a serious recession, lost jobs, people without work or income yet payments to be made, extended school closures amid a rampant and escalating pandemic, police shootings of people of color, peaceful protests often accompanied by violence in the streets, and what some would deem the most consequential presidential election of our time. Life for too many seemed at the least dismal, if not hopeless. The years 2021 and 2022 were somewhat improved yet a cloud of darkness often remained—specifically with the advent of virus variants, extended unemployment, and continued school openings and subsequent closures.

A 2020 Gallup survey revealed a new high of 65% of Americans viewing conditions in the United States as getting worse, while 23% felt life was becoming better. Consequently, close to three-fourths of adults surveyed expected a level of despair, despondency, and pessimism, as a result of the pandemic and associated repercussions, as well as turbulent politically-motivated activism, to persist for years to come (Saad, 2020).

Much of this despair flows over into classrooms all across the nation. Principals must recognize the hard-edged implications of hopelessness and pessimism. While hope and optimism seem to many as soft concepts, both are much more related to the human psyche than often realized. Hope and optimism are the basis of all positive change because both represent what could be better. Principals must keep both alive and avoid the clumsy obstacles and processes that will obstruct teaching and learning. Hope and optimism involve a principal and team taking positive thoughts about the future and placing human, fiscal, and material resources and dedicated efforts (hard work) into a leadership framework to best ensure positive progress occurs. How? By what means?

First, principals must ensure student and teacher engagement. There is a strong link or correlation between hope and engagement. Principals must exude optimism and hopefulness. They must help students and teachers engage in teaching and learning. Engagement is an essential component of feeling hopeful about the future. Principals must be passionate about today, tomorrow, and the future and work to impress this optimism upon other members of the learning community. Hope and optimism boost quality, engagement, productivity, peace of mind, and overall well-being. Creating an atmosphere of interest, eagerness, excitement, and optimism about schooling is a hallmark of hopeful leadership.

Second, principals must create an open culture and positive climate—a culture and climate of enthusiasm. Enthusiasm is the result of inspiration. Principals inspire enthusiasm in students and teachers by collaboratively developing meaningful goals, by being excited about being a part of the learning community, and by rallying students and team members in service for a better way—always encouraging a "can do" spirit. These principals are honest, transparent, student-centered, hopeful, and celebratory.

Third, principals must model, coach, and teach hopefulness and optimism. Principals have to ask an all-important question: "What excites you about school, what are you learning that inspires you, and what motivates you about the work we are doing?" Then, a follow-up query must be voiced: "What are you contributing to your excitement, to that something which is bigger than yourself?" Then, remind all members of the learning community, "We are capable of generating hope. We are deeply invested in knowing where we are, where we can be, and how we can get there and make life, teaching, and learning better!"

Hope ensures a strong, positive, and balanced well-being. Hope makes tough situations more bearable. Hope motivates individuals to take steps toward a brighter future. Hope provides people with a mindset to strive and succeed. Hope increases the chances for goal accomplishment. Hope leads to improvement. Hope enables individuals to look forward to a positive outcome in studies, career, and life. Hope is the belief that circumstances will improve—not a wish that things will get better but an actual belief, an acknowledgement that all will be reclaimed and regained, no matter how great or minute, notable or ordinary, exalted or modest, wonderful or dreadful, important or trivial. Hope fuels optimism and opportunity. When abandoned in life, there must always be hope! Some would reply, "Easier said than done! How can I hope and cope in times of little hope?"

COPING STRATEGIES ARE ESSENTIAL FOR THE WELL-BEING OF THE LEARNING COMMUNITY

Simply put, life today is not easy for anyone—especially in learning communities where members can often feel discarded, degraded, disenfranchised, and/or hopeless. Stress, anxiety, depression, burdensome lifestyles, home issues, school problems, pandemics, bullies, suicides, rampant dysfunction, racism, inequities and inequalities, bigotry, and politics of hate serve as a list that is just the tip of the proverbial iceberg. Sometimes it seems like members of the human race have little or no control over personal thoughts, feelings, and the stresses and worries of everyday life. Yet, psychological help with associated strategies and patterns of behavior is available to minimize or mitigate the emotional strains of living.

What coping mechanisms and/or skills, so essential to the well-being of a learning community, are available? First, to better understand how emotional well-being can be attained, a working definition of "coping" must be identified. Coping is a basic process integral to adaptation and survival. Coping is all about people detecting, appraising, handling, and learning from stressful encounters which occur across the spectrum of a lifetime (Zimmer-Gembeck & Skinner, 2016).

Coping strategies, as further defined, or described in the next section of this chapter, are models or practices by which an individual or groups of individuals can think in different ways to solve a predicament to include but not limited to problem-solving, information-seeking, cognitive-restructuring, emotional expression, distraction and avoidance, wishful-thinking, social support, and overall acceptance (Dubow & Rubinlicht, 2011). Coping is all about surviving in a world that is quite often nonsurvivable.

Coping mechanisms, methods, models, styles, skills, strategies, and/or practices are as numerous and varied as these incorporated terms and the stressors that precede them. Identified below is a TOP-10 listing of coping strategies that individuals within and across a learning community can incorporate.

TOP-10 Coping Strategies: A Second Treatment Leading to a Cure

These coping strategies are adaptable to students, teachers, principals, and parents and range from coping with stress to forms of psychological well-being; to testing; to health, gender identification, sexual orientation; to other worrisome problems; to issues of life; and to emotion-stressing changes in life. Each strategy listed below applies to any age. Just incorporate any one or more of these strategies when working with students or parents or any members of the learning community.

1. *Increase self-esteem.* Having a healthy self-esteem aids in coping with the struggles of life and helps students, faculty, staff, and others overcome negative thoughts and feelings. How does one increase self-esteem? Try these identified boosters. Individuals can:
   - do something they love and enjoy
   - keep a journal of positives that occur each day
   - unfollow social media accounts that cause worsening feelings
   - compliment others. Compliments will be returned
   - set small, attainable goals for each day or week (Young Minds, 2019)

2. *Be mindful.* Help members of the learning community practice the focusing of attention and awareness on the now. Mindfulness is being present in the moment. It is a state or quality of being conscious or aware of something in the present. Here are a few examples, as identified by the Mayo Clinic (2018), that can be employed:
   - Pay attention. It's hard to slow down and notice things in a busy world. Try to take the time to experience the surrounding environment with all of the senses: touch, sound, sight, smell, and taste.
   - Yawn and stretch for 10 seconds every hour.
   - Stand and breathe, deliberately, in and out.
   - Discharge any unpleasant sensations, emotions, or feelings.
   - Take notice of pleasant sensations, emotions, or feelings.
   - Observe the surroundings. Detect something about the environment that is pleasant and be grateful for what is noticed.
   - Ask these questions: What are the possibilities? What is a new step forward?
   - Think of something or someone that is loving and kind.

   Mindfulness reduces anxiety, stress, and depression (Psychology Today, 2019). Moreover, mindfulness can be utilized by individuals of all ages and from differing backgrounds who are suffering from differing problems. There is mindful breathing, mindful observation, and mindful listening. Mindfulness is all about being aware of what is happening in the present moment and then overcoming any worrisome factors. Guide students, for example, to the following website for 25 fun mindfulness activities as proposed by Ackerman (2020): https://positivepsychology.com/mindfulness-for-children-kids-activities/.
3. *Encourage them to talk and share.* People who share what is bothering them find life more manageable. When an individual feels life's problems are overwhelming, talk and share with someone—a physician, therapist, priest, rabbi, minister, teacher, school counselor, friend, family member, principal, or someone who is trusted. Those who are not certain as to how to initiate a conversation about a personal problem simply need to open up and talk. Recall what Dr. Frasier Crane stated in each episode of the classic television comedy series *Frasier*: "I'm listening." Remember, there are people who care and really want to listen!
4. *Engage in positive self-talk.* Teachers, principals, and parents—especially when working with students—must permit said students to have a voice by giving them time and reasons to talk positively about themselves. Teachers must compliment student achievements, big and small, and share why each student is great. Every student has a greatness that needs to be identified and talked about. Let students self-talk about

their special attribute. Students know what their specific greatness is, and with a little encouragement and a reminder of said skill or strength, students will be motivated to share. The same can be said of adults.
5. *Model Positive Coping Behaviors.* Principals and teachers should not only share experiences and benefits from coping strategies, but model them to students! Model and teach coping skills such as those indicated in Textbox 1.1. Also, as a principal, confide about times when it has been personally difficult to cope. Then, share positive strategies that worked. Such a practice helps others overcome their own feelings of being out there alone with a struggle they believe no one else has experienced or felt.
6. *Stay engaged and connected.* Social interaction and activism improves both physical and mental health as well as emotional well-being. Encourage all members of the learning community, certainly students, to interact face-to-face with a friend, a family member, or someone that is or can become a trusted confidant. Social media is fine but often has troublesome consequences. Social interaction, however, when face-to-face is better and most essential to an individual's well-being. Social activism helps overcome the inequities and inequalities so persistent in far too many lives—especially for peoples of color.
7. *Listen to soothing music.* Music is a powerful, medically proven method to improving the well-being of students and adults. The positive effects of music are well documented and include stress management, lowering blood pressure, decreasing stress hormones, aiding clinical depression, and even benefiting bipolar disorder (Harvard Health Publishing, 2011). Students and faculty, too, who play soothing music anywhere at any time are emotionally better. The results are amazing. Listed are a couple of links to oldies but goldies from the 1970s. Okay, let out a chuckle, and then, take the bait. Give in and listen. The music will soothe anyone into a state of positive well-being. Guaranteed!
   - https://www.youtube.com/watch?v=MEO6gYCFbr0 ("Sailing" by Christopher Cross, 1979)
   - https://www.youtube.com/watch?v=14pitnJlcv4 ("Breezin'" by George Benson, 1976)
8. *Sing.* Singing, much like listening to music, has been scientifically proven to lower stress; relieve anxiety; and elevate endorphins, which create happiness and well-being (Hunt, 2019). Singing relaxes muscle tension, decreases stress hormones in the bloodstream, and takes a weary mind off the troubles of the day. Singing is a source of eminent pleasure and immediately invigorates. Recall the words, in verse, of "Sing" by the Carpenters. Even better, simply do an Internet search and listen to the song. Students, too, should be encouraged to sing, even in class (when appropriate, of course), and even when a terrible voice,

TEXTBOX 1.1. EXAMPLES OF HOW TO MODEL AND TEACH COPING SKILLS TO STUDENTS

Principals and teachers, when modeling and teaching coping skills, must:

- Maintain daily routines to the extent possible.
- Provide structured time to talk about the event.
- Be alert to expressions of overwhelming feelings.
- Provide a sense of security, familiarity, and comfort.
- Remind students that they are safe at school.
- Plan classroom and campus interventions collaboratively with counselors.
- Meet individually with students, as required.
- Openly and honestly discuss the event with students.
- Share with students that talking about events of life is central to well-being.
- Permit students to plan and structure a special activity. Student sense of control is a major coping mechanism.
- Recognize changes in students' usual or normal behavior. Such changes are often resulting factors/consequences of trauma, stress, inequities, or inequalities.
- Acknowledge questions about death and/or destruction.
- Recognize student feelings—sad, angry, worried, etc.
- Lead discussions that will help students gain a sense of security and understanding.
- Understand the importance of peer interactions as a means of coping.
- Expect and handle emotional swings. For teenagers, their cognitive abilities are often greater than their emotional capacity to manage highly stressful situations.
- Help students reframe their expressions of rage or despair. Focus on helping students to find positive, well-being solutions such as coordinating memorial ceremonies or special school assemblies or donating time and creativity to fundraising or blood drives.

bad pitch, or offbeat tone is the case. Students will feel better. Again, guaranteed!
9. *Laugh*. Everyone needs to find that one individual who makes them laugh. Then, they need to let out a belly laugh and feel better! Turn on the television or cell phone or laptop or tablet at home and find a really

funny television show, comedian, or comedy special, or even a silly movie. Laughter is truly the best medicine when it comes to well-being!
10. *Serve.* Negativity is an emotional state of being that creates a downward spiral by means of an inward retreating process. Negativity creates worry, stress, anxiety, and depression. Studies reveal that helping others by serving others is not only a distractor from personal problems but makes for a positive difference in the lives of self and others. Students, for example, when serving others increase personal self-esteem and well-being (Agathangelou, 2015). Encourage students to volunteer and to also engage in social activism. Develop "at-school" and "community-oriented" volunteer projects for students. Service makes a difference, and students will feel good about it!

Heng (2018) identifies additional coping strategies to include 1) *developing self-reliance* (relying on internal resources such as learning techniques (practice, memorization, multi-tasking, talking to teachers, reaching out to peers, forming study groups), 2) *working harder/spending more time on studies* (preparing for class; minimizing procrastination; using learning centers, labs, tutorial sessions, and libraries; and engaging in extra-curricular activities), and 3) *using a range of technological/learning support systems* (educationally related Internet searches, positively/appropriately leveraging social media, incorporating software/hardware).

Naturally, other coping mechanisms such as monitoring diet, exercising, relaxation techniques, active engagement, enjoying creative expression, spirituality, adopting a pet, sleeping, avoiding certain foods, and even taking prescribed medications or supplements can be taught, modeled, and encouraged.

Important Note: This chapter serves as an introduction to the subject of well-being and its relationship to every member of the learning community. What follows in Chapter 2 is a detailed guide or approach for principals when attempting to develop a successful "How-To" well-being program.

CONCLUDING COMMENTS

Principals, never forget self! School leaders need well-being support, too, in order to flourish. Often selfless in deeds and actions, principals are those on-campus transformative individuals who set the tone, establish the school climate and culture, and on whom the success of students, faculty, and instructional programs, initiatives, and activities rest. It's a load—all too frequently, a heavy load!

To better ensure the school principal is emotionally, socially, and mentally prepared for the crucial role of leading, Superville (2021) recommends the following considerations: 1) take a self-administered protocol (see Chapter 7 of this text), 2) target and engage in job-specific professional development, 3) establish and take one wellness (not sick leave) day a semester, 4) seek out veteran principals as mentors, and 5) engage like-minded or similarly-situated principal colleagues. Don't be stigmatized by personal care. It makes for a better-minded school leader!

FINAL THOUGHTS

Exceptional principals work to enact Principal Action #1: Find a Cure for the ills of schooling today. Doing so, these principals recognize the difference between wellness and well-being, noting that well-being is all about the positive emotions and moods exuded within and across a learning community. The well-being of all members of the learning community is about pleasure, joyfulness, and satisfaction, absent the negative emotions of depression, anxiety, dejection, sadness, and hopelessness. These same principals also understand how the prevailing winds of dismay can push through a school, leaving behind an affliction that must be addressed and cured.

Exceptional principals know the significance of modeling and promoting emotional well-being, not only relative to students but to all members of the learning community—faculty and staff, parents, community members, and business leaders. Sheila Robinson-Kiss (2020) reminds principals and team members that neglecting the mental health of a community of learners can be lethal. The very best principals share and incorporate coping strategies essential for the well-being of their learning communities.

Such strategies include: 1) taking advantage of free therapy on campus, online, and pro bono; 2) emptying, daily, emotional stress and strain, which compounds teaching, leading, and learning; 3) finding and engaging an accountability friend; 4) monitoring diet, exercising regularly, and relaxing; 5) increasing self-esteem; 6) incorporating mindfulness: focusing attention and awareness of the positives of now; 7) sharing the overwhelmingness of life with another: finding a friend or accountability buddy who will listen, empathize, and offer guidance; 8) engaging in activities to take the mind off the trials and tribulations of being human; 9) staying engaged, busy, and connected—socially interacting; and 10) doing those things that make for a happy life (spirituality, music, singing, laughing, serving, and even sleeping).

DISCUSSION QUESTIONS

1. When examining Principal Action #1: Find a Cure, why is well-being a better definition and application as opposed to wellness in schools?

2. What is the ever-pervading affliction described in this chapter and why is it a problem worthy of Principal Action #1: Find a Cure? How can this affliction be solved?
3. Of the three leadership framework strategies for a principal to promote hope and optimism in schools, which one do you perceive to be the most effective when working with students? What about faculty and staff?
4. Consider the TOP-10 coping strategies identified in the chapter. Which strategy have you, personally, implemented this school year? Identify the circumstance and then contemplate what other chapter-noted coping strategies could help create a stronger, healthier environment of well-being, hope, and optimism.
5. Carefully examine the TOP-10 coping strategies and identify which might best apply to a principal working with Chanice Kobolowski, the teacher in the earlier "Making Peace with Trouble" scenario?
6. How do the TOP-10 coping strategies correlate with Principal Action #1: Find a Cure and the overall well-being of a learning community, as perceived through the lenses of hope and optimism?

CASE STUDY APPLICATION: DO WE REALLY MATTER?

School principal Alma Parker and counselor Halcyon Maxwell for several weeks had been interacting and conversing with one of the school's students, Neva Tremaine, who came from a troubled home: an abusive stepfather, an uninterested if not uncaring mother, and an innocent and much younger sibling who was not old enough to recognize the trials and tribulations that befell his older sister. Her nearest and favorite relative, her maternal grandmother, lived 500 miles away. This late afternoon, Neva was once again in the principal's office following the dismissal of school.

Neva Tremaine was a smart young lady—a straight A student who was articulate and capable of going far in life. Yet, Neva was troubled, living in the midst of a troubled life. School counselor Maxwell regularly provided therapeutic sessions for Neva. The counselor openly admitted to Principal Parker that while she was neither a psychologist nor a psychiatrist, she believed that Neva was a student in the grips of serious clinical depression—compounded even more so by her home environment. This particular afternoon, while speaking with Principal Parker, Neva said, "You know, Ms. Parker, we're no more than a teeny, tiny, infinitesimal blip in this life. Do we really matter?"

Principal Parker responded by saying, "We do, Neva. We matter because we are not meaningless. We are not necessarily here on earth to make money or live a lavish lifestyle. We matter because we have in us the hope for and optimism of love. We may not sense love from others, but we can, ourselves, love and care for each other, deeply and affectionately. Our well-being is not necessarily predicated on who loves us but on who we love."

Principal Parker then noted, "Neva, life is transient. In many respects, life is a series of events or periods that are fleeting, periods that will come and go. Life is a series of transitory phases—some good, some bad. But as individuals, we must always be optimistic. What you are experiencing today can very well be overshadowed by acts of compassion, love, care, and devotion tomorrow.

"Neva, dear," the principal stated, "the future holds so much good, hope, and positiveness in store for you. Your well-being as an individual can be in your hands and appropriately and effectively managed by you. You are able to guide and direct your life by making good choices, and appropriate decisions. Yes, others may interfere. Others may even take advantage of and hurt you, but ultimately, you are in control of your own destiny."

The principal then shared, "Plus, along your path through this life, you will find those who will not only care for you, such as Ms. Maxwell and myself, but that someone special, in the future, who will ultimately love and deeply care for you. Neva, your well-being, your hope for a better tomorrow is at your fingertips. Reach out, grasp, and hold on to those who will help you, those who will guide and advise you, and those who will love and appreciate you for who you are and for who you will become, and who recognize what you are capable of doing today, tomorrow, and in the future."

Principal Parker closed the late afternoon session by reminding Neva, "You do matter. Your life matters—more than you may realize today. Continue your sessions with Ms. Maxwell. Oh, and Neva, recall the old saying 'Hope springs eternal!' Remember, Neva, we are here for you!"

APPLICATION QUESTIONS

1. How is Principal Action #1: Find a Cure and well-being applicable to this case study? To student Neva Tremaine? To the principal and school counselor? Explain.
2. Consider the three bulleted supportive mental and emotional health service options, as identified in the chapter. Which one of the three options might best help Neva Tremaine and her well-being?
3. Reexamine each of the three leadership framework strategies for a principal to promote hope and optimism in schools. Which one of the three strategies could best assist Neva Tremaine and her overall well-being?

4. TOP-10 coping strategies: Which apply to this case study? Robbins and Judge (2019) in their classic 18th edition text, *Organizational Behavior: Concepts, Controversies, and Applications,* address four coping strategies for individuals: 1) time management, 2) physical exercise, 3) relaxation training, and 4) social support. Which of the TOP-10 coping strategies as addressed in the chapter correlate with the four as identified by Robbins and Judge? How do those you have identified apply to this particular case study and, more importantly, to the student, Neva Tremaine? Be detailed in your explanation.
5. Consider this statement made by Neva Tremaine: "You know, Ms. Parker, we're no more than a teeny, tiny, infinitesimal blip in this life. Do we really matter?" and then, answer the following questions:
    - Is the statement more than a call for a therapeutic talk or guidance session? Explain and expound upon your response.
    - How is Principal Action #1: Find a Cure applicable to this statement made by Neva Tremaine: "We're no more than a teeny tiny infinitesimal blip in this life" and what's a principal to do?

Chapter 2

Principal Action #2

Develop a Successful Well-Being Program

THE "HOW-TO" FOR ADVANCING AN EFFECTIVE WELL-BEING CURRICULUM

"Without continual growth and development, words such as improvement, achievement, and success have no meaning."—Benjamin Franklin (BrainyQuote, 2020)

"Success is no accident. It is hard work, perseverance, learning, studying, sacrifice, and most of all, love of what you are doing or learning to do!"—Unattributed

WHAT'S NEXT? OR WHAT ARE YOU DOING, NOW?

During a recent high school graduation, the keynote speaker asked the inevitable question frequently asked of graduating seniors: "What's next?" Then, the speaker said, "What's next is important, but here's a much more essential, if not critical, question: 'What are you doing, now?'" An excellent, if not thought-provoking, query! Principals must always ask the "what's next?" question but never forget to ask the "What are you doing, now?" query of themselves, of their faculty, and of their students.

From a more direct principal-oriented perspective, here are 20 reflective, if not pointed and revealing, "What are you doing, now?" inquiries. Are you, as a school leader:

1. practicing honesty, now?
2. developing relationships, now?
3. leading with integrity, now?
4. utilizing good judgment, now?
5. engaging empathetically, now?
6. offering honorable guidance, now?
7. making good decisions, now?
8. leading and learning, now?
9. avoiding temptations, now?
10. listening to others, now?
11. averting inequities and inequalities, now?
12. being open-minded, now?
13. being slow to anger, now?
14. taking corrective actions, now?
15. establishing a good reputation, now?
16. avoiding past mistakes, now?
17. collaborating with others, now?
18. surrounding yourself with competent individuals, now?
19. using past experiences as good guidance, now?
20. showing others "how to" develop a culture of well-being, now?

The "What's next?" question must always be accompanied by the "What are you doing, now?" query if a principal honestly intends to develop a culture of well-being, which is the critical and initial step that is inextricably tied to social and emotional learning, equity, and equality in a democratic classroom and society. But first, the "how-to" part.

HOW TO PROMOTE THE PRACTICE OF WELL-BEING

First, principals and faculty can do better in the promotion and practice of well-being in schools. Second, there must be a genuine focus on improvement. Third, a more balanced approach must be rendered between well-being and academic achievement. For years, the major focus (the sole focus in some schools) has been state testing and accountability standards and practices. Limited, if not little, effort has been afforded to the well-being of students, faculty, parents, and other members of the learning community.

Fourth, the federal government, state legislatures, and local districts must fund additional layers of support at the school-site level, to include the hiring of additional campus counselors (DeMatthews, 2019). According to Good Docs (2020), nationwide, the typical school counselor-to-student ratio is 1 to 490, and it's worse in schools serving students of poverty and color. Fifth, students must be the focus or center of attention when it comes to their well-being. Lip service has far too often been a constant when it comes to the well-being of students. Sixth, equity and equality must be emphasized and incorporated into campus culture as daily norms. Seventh, the understanding of another's feelings (empathy) serves to deepen relationships within and across the learning community. These seven "how-to" measures help promote the practice of well-being.

Principals and teams at schools that promote well-being and wish to initiate Principal Action #2: Develop a Successful Well-Being Program reveal a common thread in practice. These school leaders and faculties work for the well-being and benefit of everyone—students as well as the entire learning community. These principals respond with very specific strategies and their focus is always addressing the well-being concerns and issues of others.

Bottom line: Schooling, today, must be improved with principals being inspired and motivated by actions to enhance every potential effort for the well-being of others. This question is regularly posed: "What restorative practices are best for all members of the learning community?" Then, a follow-up query must be addressed: "How and by what means?"

The How: Develop a Culture of Well-Being

A culture of well-being must be established based on restorative approaches to not only address accountability standards and testing but social and emotional healing and the well-being of others. A culture of well-being is one in which a principal ensures positive, helpful, and healing values that are visible, cherished, and explicitly driven as a part of school operations and practices. A culture of well-being is all about promoting the strengths and potentials of everyone: students, teachers, parents, and community members. A culture of well-being is based on the attitude that the encouraging and seeking of help is beneficial. This attitude must be an exhibited campus norm.

How to Promote and Develop a Learning Community and Culture of Well-Being

It has been said that the opposite of well-being is downtrodden. Principals must address the elephant in the room with the following question: "Is our campus downtrodden?" If this question is posed and a principal is serious in seeking an answer, the following, regrettably, are negative indicators that must be addressed:

- Increased levels of suspensions and lockdowns

- Attendance rates below the district and state standards of excellence
- Failure rates at alarming degrees—anything above 10 percent
- Student mobility rates and reasons ignored
- Students (following the direction of parents) fleeing the campus attendance zone
- Graffiti and a poorly maintained school and learning environment exist.
- Inequities and inequalities are tolerated or prevail.
- Empathy is a circumvented if not shunned practice.
- What's best for the adults, not students, on campus is the priority.
- The views of students, parents, teachers, and other members of the learning community are negative and uncaring at worst, relaxed and troubling at best.
- The positives of schooling and the well-being of others, as addressed in the research literature and showcased in other district schools, remain ignored.
- The seeking of support for and funding to improve and develop an open culture and positive learning environment is disregarded.

If any *one* of these 10 indicators, as identified by Govorova, Benitez, and Muniz (2020) and Sorenson and Goldsmith (2018), applies, then well-being *is not* a campus focus. Principals must properly, effectively, and morally lead. Failure to do so is a resulting, if not a damning, school leadership characteristic and descriptor.

Principal Responsibilities for Developing a Successful Well-Being Program

Principals must be responsible for establishing, developing, and designing a successful well-being program and serving as strong advocates for the implementation and improvement of campus-level well-being models (as noted in Textbox 2.1). Such responsibility and advocacy relate to teaming and relationship building, regular well-being meetings, and the sharing and strengthening of well-being strategies to impact students and other members of the learning community, both effectively and positively. Such relationship development processes provide opportunities for the teaching and learning of well-being activities.

Principals must work with teachers to maintain the evolvement of initiated well-being strategies and models. Principals must support ongoing dialogue to build group consensus measures, establish well-being processes, review associated expectations, and improve the overall performance of a school's well-being practices. Principals must recognize that the development of sustainable well-being strategies, models, and systems requires their own skillful leadership.

TEXTBOX 2.1. HOW TO ESTABLISH A WELL-BEING PROGRAM

To best establish a well-being program, principals must:

1. Conduct Assessments:
   - Student, faculty, and parent surveys assessing current campus climate.
   - Examine the well-being programs of other district, region, and state schools to determine a best-fit for the campus.
   - Review and evaluate current well-being plan.
2. Ensure District Support:
   - Ascertain the district's short- and long-range strategic well-being priorities.
   - Identify district supervisor(s), leadership styles and willingness to engage and support a campus well-being program.
3. Establish a Well-Being Committee:
   -
   - Committee responsibilities must include:
     - evaluating the current program or the newly initiated/piloted well-being program and assessing student needs and preferences
     - developing an ongoing operational plan to include vision or mission statement
     - assisting in the program implementation as well as frequent (monthly) monitoring and evaluation of student well-being activities
4. Develop Goals and Objectives:
   -
   -
   - Utilize information gathered from surveys and assessments to establish programmatic goals and specific well-being objectives. Examples of goals or objectives could include:
     - Reduce the number of _____ by ___ percent during the 20__ school year.
     - Increase the number of students enrolled/participating in _____ classes by ___ percent by the conclusion of the first six weeks of school.
     - Decrease the number of students identified as at risk of _____ by ___ percent during the 20__ school year.

- Increase student adherence and participation in the well-being program and/or instructional and/or extra-curricular activities by ___%.
5. Create a Fiscal/Community Lifeline:
    - Establish a well-being program "line item" as part of the school budget as a means of supporting and promoting programmatic/student success.
    - Research free community well-being resources to supplement the campus well-being program.
6. Communicate the Well-Being Plan:
    -
    -
    - Promote and market the campus/student well-being program.
        - Attention-generating program rollout utilizing multiple avenues of communication such as e-mails, social media, fliers, posters, announcements, and presentations.
        - Well-being program logo and slogan(s).
        - Visible endorsement/participation by principal and teachers.
        - Well-being plan based on research-based, student-centered best practices.
        - Persuade participation based on anecdotal situations.
        - Sustain the well-being message by making it part of the curriculum and instructional program.
        - Freshen the well-being message with new and relevant information and activities to better ensure student participation.
        - Repetition of the well-being program initiative and message to ensure programmatic focus and student interest.
        - Regularly (daily) explain/promote why social and emotional health is valued.
7. Evaluate Programmatic Success:
    - Measure the effectiveness of the well-being program.
    - Establish programmatic metrics and baselines.
    - Revise and update the program, always implementing new and research-based initiatives and activities.

Sources: Society for Human Resources Management 2021; and Sorenson & Goldsmith (2021).

Consistency in training and implementing well-being strategies and models is another principal responsibility essential to best supporting the cohesion of the greater learning community. The consistency of training and implementation must be monitored by a principal. Moreover, data must be gathered, analyzed, and ultimately shared at team meetings. The analyzed data, and associated actions required, aid a principal and team in fine-tuning the continued implementation of well-being procedures and practices via student-oriented activities.

Finally, principals are responsible for surveying students and their families, as well as faculty, to determine how the well-being experience is progressing. Surveys should include the following questions:

1. Are members of the learning community experiencing a sense of belonging?
2. Are students and faculty feeling more safe and secure within the instructional setting?
3. Has the school culture and climate improved?
4. Are aspects of the school's curriculum as well as faculty, staff, and administration promoting a deeper understanding of culturally responsive and well-being practices?
5. Has the experience improved engagement and achievement outcomes as reflected in improved feelings of well-being and related effects? In other words, does the survey process reveal overall student feelings of positive well-being?

The "How": The "Key" to Improving Student Well-Being and Overcoming a Pandemic State of Mind

The "key" to understanding "how" students have been negatively impacted, in multiple ways and specifically by, for example, the COVID-19 virus, is to examine the research literature. Many experts believe the negative impact of COVID-19 continues to this day and will continue for years well beyond the pandemic itself. UNESCO, for example, has suggested that the COVID-19 pandemic has already had a devastating impact on children in low socioeconomic communities, especially female students. Such negativity is measured by numerous indicators, specifically six adverse impact indicators (UNESCO, 2021).

Negative impact indicators that principals and teams must be aware of are what Gupta and Jawanda (2020) have identified as:

1. effects on education (widening of learning and achievement gaps).
2. anxiety about the future (delays in examinations, graduations, school openings, and the start of life work; continued virus variants or other pandemic diseases).

3. aggressive behavioral changes (isolation, loneliness, and missed interactions have deprived students and have led to drastic behavioral changes and challenges).
4. lack of a social environment (social disconnection hampers psychological and personal development).
5. addiction to social media and the Internet (students were actively encouraged to go online by schools, thus becoming not only a means of education but a disturbing distraction with a high-risk potential for students to become exposed to inappropriate content and cyberbullying.
6. increased risk of child mistreatment, abuse, and neglect (increase of child labor, domestic and child abuse, and even sexual exploitation).
7. Inequities and inequalities are tolerated, if not abused. Empathy is absent in social and emotional intercourse.

What was required then of principals and school teams and continues today is a supportive network to better ensure the well-being of students during and after any health or other crisis. Such support structures are "key" to understanding "how" principals and teams must react to the well-being of students. They call for:

- continued conversations regarding health and social issues, as well as relationships associated with student well-being
- increased emotional and social support for students during and after a crisis
- improved school and district mental health support resources
- support of students, families, and faculties as a result of crisis struggles
- increased therapeutic practices relative to traumatic events (loss of friends and loved ones)

The pandemic has proved, beyond a shadow of a doubt, to be a series of valuable and at times surprising if not shocking learning experiences for principals, teachers, students, parents, and politicians. Uncertainty and disruption have continually prevailed since the early spring months of 2020 through the most recent school year. The toll—relative to the well-being of students, teachers, and even principals—has been far too often tragic.

WELL-BEING IN THE CURRICULUM

Well-being, as a major aspect of a school's curriculum, effectively places students and their development as learners at the center of what education is intended to do: Ensure that students feel safe, secure, and are thus able to achieve as learners. Principals who lead schools with effective well-being practices recognize how essential the explicit teaching of well-being is to the success of all students.

These principals promote teaching and learning practices that enable students to become caring, inclusive, and cohesive learners. Well-being practices of effective instruction and values-based education/learning must be inclusions within a school's curriculum. Leaders, teachers, and students must be active deliverers and learners of, as well as engagers in, well-being practices and, moreover, serve as models for said practices.

Curriculum which promotes well-being serves to guide principals in leading their teaching staff to:
- nurture student dispositions (persistence, tenacity, and personal and confident identities, for example) to better support learning
- teach students how to support the learning of self and peers
- exhibit to students a care for learning
- demonstrate a pedagogy that values and honors diversity, cultural differences, equity, equality, and appropriate civic engagement
- support student activism via students sharing personal, yet opposite views, ideas, and understandings
- incorporate debate as opposed to assertion to solve and resolve conflicts in learning, achieving, and society
- organize a learning environment by properly and appropriately grouping students and designing and implementing learning activities which better develop an inclusive learning community

Principals must recognize that well-being cannot stand alone. Well-being must be woven into and across the curriculum by means of a responsive curriculum. Well-being must be embedded into a school's curriculum, instructional program, and subject areas as this learning process is critical to forming, developing, challenging, and changing how students learn and succeed academically, emotionally, socially, and behaviorally.

A Responsive Curriculum

Principals must lead and coach teachers in developing appropriate skills to develop classroom instruction that accounts for student strengths, interests, and needs. This approach to learning may very well be different in various classrooms, all depending on the teacher, and on students' abilities and learning levels. This type of curriculum moves toward a democratic classroom where students advocate for themselves, their learning styles, and their own goals. In a responsive curriculum, teachers are much more apt to establish workshop approaches to learning. Who leads a workshop? A teacher, or an individual student, or a guest expert.

Within a responsive curricular setting, teachers negotiate with students the units of learning and associated academic experiences. Instructional programs and activities offer students a choice in forms of assessment, learning tasks, subject topics, units, and how knowledge and skills are acquired. Here, students can respond to learning activities in a variety of genres, models, and approaches.

The responsive curriculum best ensures that student suggestions, contributions, and needs are:

- invited, accepted, and incorporated
- valued by teachers through verbal responses and teacher practices
- met through modified work units and supportive learning activities and instructional procedures

Leadership teams (principal, assistant principals, academic coaches, lead teachers) must monitor classroom learning to include talking with students to determine their understanding of the instructional process and how such is impacting their own learning and well-being. An established set of questions can be developed and incorporated as discussion starters to include but not limited to the following:

- What does your teacher do to assist you with your learning?
- What does your teacher do that gets in the way of your learning?
- Do you have certain goals for yourself that your teacher is not aware of?

These questions are not designed to serve as "gotcha" moments or as a means of teacher entrapment. Not at all. The student responses to such queries are to be analyzed and catalogued to best identify specific themes and certain patterns. Once identified, a member of the leadership team will interact with a teacher and positively share the findings. Such findings will best serve not only the teacher and the instructional process, but the students and their well-being.

Additionally, the results of the student queries can be seismic with important shifts within and across the curriculum. The curriculum is no longer static but ever-changing—all for the benefit and well-being of the students served. Consequently, a class may be structured around a series of workshops and one-on-one conferencing opportunities. This is responsive learning.

Responsive Instruction: An Examination

Responsive instruction is all about teaching practices which create classrooms that are democratic and safe for students to explore, negotiate, practice trial and error, and take risks in their acquisition of knowledge. Responsive instruction makes the well-being of students a priority. It engages students, teachers, and administrative team members in joyful, appealing, interactive, and helpful learning environments where the development of student well-being focuses not only on academics, but on social and emotional aspects of achievement.

Responsive instruction establishes a set of academic competencies which include cooperation, assertiveness, responsibility, empathy, dependability, perseverance, tenacity, and leadership capacity. These learned skills and behaviors are strongly correlated with social interaction, and the integration of academic and social-emotional practices whereby the shared practices, as noted in Textbox 2.2, establish responsive classrooms.

Responsive instruction is a means of teaching and learning by which the well-being of students is a first and foremost consideration, not an afterthought. Students are more involved, engaged, and participative, not only in curricular decision-making, but in making positive instructional contributions to their own personal learning. Student voice in the instructional process suddenly becomes resounding in tone, volume, and practice.

FINAL THOUGHTS

Exceptional principals initiate Principal Action #2: Develop a Successful Well-Being Program by creating a culture which promotes collaboration, student-centeredness, the spreading of common values and beliefs such as the inclusion of student voice, shared expectations, and the establishment of common ground between school and home, teachers and parents, and students and teachers.

Exceptional principals take responsibility for the well-being of all students and every member of the learning community by advocacy, teaming, relationship building, meeting and discussing and problem-solving, and sharing and strengthening well-being strategies that positively impact students and other members of the learning community. These same principals commit to consistency in the training of faculty and students relative to specific well-being strategies which build support, cohesion, and a student-first agenda.

Exceptional principals, working collaboratively with teachers, students, and parents, develop a well-being curriculum which promotes the nurturing of student dispositions, teaches students how to engage in self- and peer learning, demonstrates a pedagogy that values and honors diversity and

TEXTBOX 2.2. SHARED PRACTICES ESTABLISH A RESPONSIVE INSTRUCTION CLASSROOM

- *Interactive Modeling.* Students learn how to properly behave and interact with others, along with responsibly give, receive, and accept feedback. Purposeful contexts and activities are developed whereby students engage in social and emotional interactive situations.
- *Teacher and Student Language.* The intentional use of language skills enables students to engage and interact with their teachers and peers all the while learning and developing academic, social, emotional, and behavioral skills essential to becoming successful members within and outside the learning community.
- *Logical Consequences.* Teachers establish clear limits regarding student misbehaviors, and when students exceed said limits, they are permitted the opportunity to change their behavior and, thus, learn from their mistakes—all the while maintaining their dignity and well-being.
- *Responsive Class Sessions.* Classroom gatherings are always predictable with established routines organized around a framework of building meaningful connections, developing respectful and trusting relationships, and addressing the developmental needs of students. Students are asked to not only engage in learning but be recognized as advisors, if not directors, in their own learning and achievement.
- *Active Learning and Teaching.* Teachers are responsible for explaining, illustrating, and modeling active and hands-on instructional content to best enable students to engage in instructional practice. Students, too, are responsible for negotiating their own learning. This practice of responsive learning is always under a teacher's guidance whereby student thinking and learning can be gauged, directed, and corrected if students are moving away from intended outcomes and skills acquisition.
- *Small-Group Interaction and Learning.* Similar to cooperative learning, students work together on specific learning goals and assignments. However, this instructional process is much more student driven in identifying what activity or project will serve as the instructional mechanism for learning and achievement.

cultural differences, and, again, incorporates student voice when solving and resolving conflicts in learning and achievement and in socialization.

Exceptional principals work with teachers, students, and parents to develop and invest in responsive instruction whereby 1) student suggestions are invited, accepted, and incorporated into the curriculum; 2) student contributions are valued by teachers through positive verbal responses and teacher practices; and 3) the individual needs of students are addressed and met by means of interactive modeling, logical consequences, respectful and trusting relationships, and the addressing of the developmental needs of all students.

Exceptional principals ensure teachers establish active learning and teaching practices along with small-group interaction and learning—all of which are at the heart of student well-being. Additionally, the very best principals promote student voice, resulting in students developing not only an energetic and engaging classroom presence, but one across campus as well. Students also become active contributors in their own instructional planning and in the revising of curriculum, instructional programming, classroom activities, and campus-wide leadership roles and responsibilities. Student views, ideas, and decision-making abilities are now heard and valued.

DISCUSSION QUESTIONS

1. What is a culture of well-being? How does such a culture improve teaching, leading, and learning as well as equity, equality, and empathy?
2. Examine the listing of negative indicators in the chapter section entitled "How to Promote and Develop a Learning Community and Culture of Well-Being," and detail which of the 12 negative indicators you have observed in your school. How can those identified negative indicators be overcome and turned into positives by principal leadership and responsibility?
3. Scrutinize the "Well-Being in the Curriculum" section of the chapter. Identified are seven "how-to" school curriculum indicators which promote well-being. Which three of the seven listed do you perceive to be the best methods of helping a principal move a school from downtrodden to well-being? Explain your reasoning.
4. What are the student benefits of responsive curriculum and instruction? Enhance your response with examples from the field of practice. How might teachers and principals benefit?

CASE STUDY APPLICATION: GUN VIOLENCE, A HELPLESS CHILD, AND THE HOPE OF A SCHOOL'S WELL-BEING PROGRAM

Angelica, a nine-year-old student at Paisano School, was playing in the street just three houses down from her family's home. She and a neighborhood friend had been riding their hand-me-down bicycles when they decided to park their bikes and sit on the curb to enjoy a cool drink from her friend's water hose. This was a typical springtime Friday evening in a neighborhood that had known its share of drive-by shootings, but never on Alameda Street, home to Angelica.

A car slowly crept down Alameda Street, a poplar tree–lined avenue, pausing only to scan a house full of party revelers that was next door to where the two young girls sat curbside. At first, neither girl paid much attention to the vehicle. Then, several teenage boys jumped out of the car and began firing a spray of bullets in the direction of the home they had scouted. Both Angelica and her friend jumped up and began to run in terror. Angelica ran directly toward her home and into the crossfire of ringing shots.

Angelica, immediately shot, was later pronounced dead at the Angel of Mercy Hospital, just a few blocks away from her home. Among the first visitors to arrive at the scene of Angelica's shooting death was Father Francis Aloysius O'Casey, priest at St. Nicholas's Church, parish to Angelica and her family. Father O'Casey provided comfort. He was most familiar with such tragic scenes and his purpose that evening was to offer help to the hopeless as they attempted to cope with the loss of a child. This was the latest of far too many senseless neighborhood shootings. Yet, Father O'Casey was always present to offer support to the families of gun violence victims.

Paisano School principal, Margarita Leos-Monsivais, soon arrived and knelt next to Father O'Casey, mourning the death of one of her students—another fatal gunshot victim. Father O'Casey turned to Principal Leos-Monsivais, as the ambulance took little Angelica and her mother to the hospital, and asked "How do you handle such grief at your school? How do you help your students cope?" The principal, already stunned by the loss of another student's life, was similarly taken aback by the father's queries.

Principal Leos-Monsivais quickly composed herself and replied: "We are a community of well-being, Father. We help our students cope with and handle the stressors of this neighborhood, of the valuable, yet sadly, devalued lives taken from this earth, way too soon. That's what we do, Father. We cope. We believe in the well-being of each other. You know, Father, a recent study revealed that a new pandemic is spreading across the nation."

The principal continued, "More than 4,600 teens and children have been victims of shootings, with more than 1,200 killed this year alone. Father, do you know that 62% of Americans have no handguns, 70% no rifles or shotguns, and 86% no assault weapons. Yet these weapons seem to get into the hands of the wrong people, at the expense of too many good people, including children.

"Across our nation," Principal Leos-Monsivais continued, "sidewalks, street corners, and sadly, schools, once bastions for fun and laughter, have become sights for vigils and memorials to mourn and remember the young lives lost to gun violence. I say enough, Father!"

Father O'Casey, further saddened, replied, "Can I stop by on Monday to learn more?" "Of course, Father," said the principal. "Call my cell phone this weekend and we can talk. Always feel free to come by the school. Monday is fine. I am so saddened by another violent gun attack, and the death of this helpless child. Father, I only hope our school's well-being program is helping our students. So many tragedies, so much trauma. You know, Father, we should have a handle on this by now."

APPLICATION QUESTIONS

1. Return to Chapter 1 and the section entitled "TOP-10 Coping Strategies." Specifically, examine 5. Model Positive Coping Behaviors and Textbox 1.1. Examples of How to Model and Teach Coping Skills Examples to Students. Of the 17 different coping behaviors listed in Textbox 1.1, which 10 would most readily apply to the circumstances noted within the case study?
2. Which of the Chapter 1 TOP-10 coping strategies, with the exception of 5. Model Positive Coping Behaviors, could best be implemented by Principal Margarita Leos-Monsivais to aid the well-being of the students at Paisano School? Illuminate and enlighten with your answer.
3. Contemplate Textbox 2.2. Shared Practices Establish a Responsive Instruction Classroom and identify which of the six practices would best apply to the case study situation. Explain why.
4. Which of the principal leadership responsibilities listed in the chapter section entitled "Principal Responsibilities for Developing a Successful Well-Being Program" correlate with this case study and Principal Action #2: Develop a Successful Well-Being Program? Clarify how and why.
5. Which curricular and instructional programs at your school serve as a means of ensuring the well-being of students? Does the example(s) identified readily represent well-being and that of a responsive

curriculum and a responsive instructional program? Be detailed in your explanation.
6. Consider the final statement of Principal Margarita Leos-Monsivais: "You know, Father, we should have a handle on this by now." What do you think is meant? Can programs of "well-being" in schools bring "well-being" to neighborhoods such as that of nine-year-old Angelica? Provide a rationale and associated reasoning relative to your answer.
7. Reexamine "The How: Develop a Culture of Well-Being" section of this chapter. What aspects of this chapter section best correlate with the case study and Principal Action #2: Develop a Successful Well-Being Program? Explain why.
8. Equity, equality, and empathy. Which of these terms are emphasized within the case study? How, by what means? Which are missing from the Paisano School and the Alameda Street community? Expound, relative to your answer/conclusion.

Chapter 3

Principal Action #3
Embrace Social and Emotional Learning

WHAT IS SOCIAL AND EMOTIONAL LEARNING (SEL) AND WHY IS IT IMPORTANT?

"Educating the mind without educating the heart is no education at all!"—Aristotle (Goodreads, 2022)

SOCIAL AND EMOTIONAL LEARNING DEFINED AND EXPLAINED

Social and emotional learning (commonly referred to as SEL in the research literature) is a process by which students, teachers, and principals acquire and apply appropriate knowledge, attitudes, and skills essential to better understanding and managing emotions—from three perspectives: personal, social, and behavioral. Principal Action #3; Embrace Social and Emotional Learning relates to establishing and achieving positive goals and outcomes not only in the school setting, but in the public arena as well. SEL is all about empathy, the establishment and maintenance of positive personal relationships, the ability to responsibly make decisions and solve problems, and the overall well-being of a learning community.

Aristotle, as noted in the opening quote, was right: Educating students is more than working with the mind. The heart, the well-being of students, must be taken into account. Therefore, it is of critical importance to understand that SEL focuses on emotional intelligence, explicit instruction, positive behavioral interventions and support, the reduction of bullying, and evidence-based programs such as Responsive Classroom, Open Circle, and RULER (recognizing, understanding, labeling, expressing, and regulating emotions). SEL works to improve the quality and character of student and teacher life. SEL improves campus culture and climate, which leads to improved and positive life outcomes (Clark, 2020).

SEL and Its Importance to Principals

Principals, for the most part, appreciate the tenets of SEL. Yet, many of their schools struggle with this educational phenomenon. Certainly, principals appreciate the teaching of skills associated with SEL. No argument! Yet, consider the following data: In 2013, only 25 percent of principals could be considered "high implementers" of SEL (Civic Enterprises and Hart Associates, 2013). In 2017, a very small increase: 33% (DePaoli, Atwell, & Bridgeland, 2017). By 2019, only 35% of principals were considered high implementers of SEL (Atwell & Bridgeland, 2019). To date, while school-based SEL programs have been shown to be effective in producing positive outcomes for students, the percentage increase of high☐implementer SEL principals has been detailed as "inconsequential" (Dowling & Barry, 2020). Encouraging? Far from it! Two questions, with answers to follow: Why the appreciation? Why the struggle?

Why the Appreciation?

Why do principals appreciate and agree with the SEL precepts? Simple explanation: SEL works! Why? It nurtures the growth and development of students when it comes to relationship skills, self-control, and mental health. SEL increases parental engagement and their understanding of schooling. SEL develops better teachers. SEL improves student functions, behaviorally and academically, in both classrooms and out-of-school settings. SEL increases student learning and achievement. SEL improves a school's culture and climate. Finally, SEL is adaptable in any type of school—rural, suburban, urban, and even online. All of the noted explanations serve as appropriate and effective reasons why principals appreciate and need SEL in their schools.

Principals, and teachers too, support SEL. A recent study released by Rand Corporation in cooperation with Hamilton and Doss (2020) produced the following findings: 1) SEL enhances confidence as related to students' social and emotional well-being; 2) there is a need for additional SEL-related professional development; 3) student, teacher, and principal well-being is higher with the incorporation of SEL practices; 4) greater levels of support exist for SEL at the elementary school level; 5) there is greater use of SEL practices if state and/or district SEL standards are in place; and 6) the use of technology to support SEL is low, especially in high-poverty schools.

Three major implications of the noted Rand study are 1) principals must address student and teacher well-being through the incorporation and utilization of SEL practices, 2) principals must equip teachers with SEL knowledge through professional development and resources (fiscal, material, and human), and 3) principals must ensure a clear instructional vision and roadmap for SEL implementation in schools.

A couple of final notes: Principals must make certain that SEL professional development is ongoing, customized, and provided by campus leaders (principal, assistant principals, and instructional coaches), and the integration of SEL instruction into the academic program requires explicit principal guidance (to include modeling lessons and related instructional methods, strategies, techniques, and activities) as well as associated resources (Schwartz et al., 2020).

Why the Struggle?

Every principal, every prospective principal, every teacher, and even parents agree on the need for more of that one elusive thing: *time*. The Civic Enterprises and Hart Associates (2013, 2017) studies reported that respondents noted that time during the course of the academic day and time for teacher training were the two greatest barriers in a principal's struggle to embrace and bring SEL to the forefront of instructional programming.

Other barriers for SEL implementation include 1) lack of funding, 2) lack of skill reinforcement at home, 3) how to measure the gaining of SEL skills, 4) lack of teacher commitment to SEL, 5) teacher resistance to change, 6) a non-priority in school districts, and 7) parents who are offended about the teaching of SEL in schools. These parents believe such skills are to be taught at home, by parents, and not in schools, by teachers. One parent recently stated, "Our family values are not to be usurped by my child's school. My husband and I will teach our child what we believe he needs in order for him to be socially and emotionally successful in life" (Sorenson, 2020a).

What's the Solution?

Consider each of the seven explanations identified below.

First, principal leadership is critical to ensuring Principal Action #3: Embrace Social and Emotional Learning is successfully initiated! Sadly, far too many principals fail to initiate curricular change or instructional initiatives for numerous reasons, but here are four that are most negatively impactful: 1) The *time* factor, again. Principals are busy. Mostly, busy with way too many meetings. But that's another topic for another day. 2) The *fear* factor. There are principals who are quite hesitant to "rock the boat" or "buck the system" for a variety of reasons. Consider the following: A principal is new in her or his role. The principal fears any initiated change will upset district office personnel/superiors or, worse, teachers. A first-year principal or even a tenured principal new to a school quite often has a steep learning curve and is fearful of wading into the deep end of the change pool. 3) The *initiative* factor. One principal recently noted, "My campus is moving along like a well-oiled machine. I don't dare make any new changes. Why should I trouble myself?" (Sorenson, 2020b). 4) The *don't understand* factor. Unfortunately, there are principals in service today who simply don't understand curriculum and instruction. They simply manage their schools. Management, while important, is by no means instructional leadership.

Principals must lead, instructionally. Recall these old and unattributed adages: "Lead, follow, or get out of the way!" "You lead by going to that place, making the case, and then, setting the pace!" "Leaders who lead are never silent!" "Great principals set out to make a difference. It's never about the role, it's always about the goal!"

Second, additional and dedicated funds are essential to best ensure the introduction, implementation, and ultimate success of SEL. In recent times, much voice has been given to "defunding police" when "defunding education" has sadly been an ongoing process since the early 2000s with little or no recognition or voice. Federal and state funding are fiscal lifelines to school districts across the nation and to the success of proven instructional programs and to the ultimate academic achievement of all students (Sorenson & Goldsmith, 2018).

Yet, for years, school funding has continuously decreased as state dollars have sharply declined, and with local funds failing to bridge the gap, not only is the economic health of schools at risk, so is the social and emotional welfare of students (Sorenson & Goldsmith, 2018). Most recently, in 2021, the COVID relief aid for education governmental funding, as part of the American Rescue Plan, emerged.

This federal funding package, for education, provides essential dollars for increased tutoring; school climate measures as related to dealing with student trauma and the avoidance of harsh or punitive punishment; innovations to include increasing instructional time, strengthening the teacher workforce, revamping curriculums, emphasizing civics instruction, and digital training and learning for teachers; as well as data systems upgrades relative to the analyses of academic outcomes; and the upgrading of outdated technological systems (LePage & Jordan, 2021).

Third, state accountability standards must be required. Specifically dictated SEL objectives and actions such as self-management, coping, goal-setting, and interpersonal and behavioral skills could be funded and enacted.

Fourth, additional research is needed regarding the positive effects of SEL, specifically, research as related to student academic achievement.

Fifth, increased training in teacher preparation programs is essential. Additionally, district pre-service (mentoring and new-teacher orientation) programming, and professional development sessions must become enhanced absolutes.

Sixth, district initiatives (curricular and instructional support) are critical to implementing SEL in schools and must begin with principal training. If student equity and equality is a goal, and it must be, districts have to be serious about SEL development in their schools. One way is for school districts to ensure that principals become trainers of trainers and that principals lead, with the assistance of academic coaches, in the training of teachers.

Seventh, the development of SEL student assessment instruments is essential as well as the inclusion of SEL as part of any teacher evaluative measures. This precept is recognized and supported by 49 percent of all principals surveyed, up from 25 percent as previously surveyed (Atwell & Bridgeland, 2019). This is a positive recognition that SEL is an effective instructional tool that best benefits students.

SEL and Its Importance to Teachers, Students, and Parents

Principals, as previously noted, are critical to successfully embracing and implementing a SEL program. Teachers, too, perform an essential role relative to the effectiveness of SEL in the classroom. If students are to achieve as a result of SEL, teacher "buy-in" is a critical key.

SEL is important to teachers because it is important to students! School, for many students, is the only place where they can gain social and emotional skills. As previously addressed, far too many parents fail to teach these essential life skills to their children because, as parents, they do not possess the social and emotional ability to do so. They, too, were never taught social and emotional skills. Identified below are four reasons why SEL instruction is important to teachers. All parties gain when teachers help students develop personal responsibility, positive self-images, better attitudes, decreased stress, and enhanced academic performance and achievement (Collaborative for Academic, Social, and Emotional Learning [CASEL], 2020).

SEL is an essential element for aiding teachers who work daily with students—many of whom are in desperate need of coping skills, especially as related to bullying and disciplinary incidents. Students who can cope help teachers cope. Students with strong social-emotional skills are better prepared to handle daily challenges, both in life and learning. Students engaged in SEL build more positive and lasting relationships, make better and more informed decisions, and solve life and school problems.

Research has revealed a positive connection between children who learn early, in school, social-emotional skills and their well-being as young adults. One study revealed that 54 percent of students who gained social-emotional skills in school were more likely to earn a high school diploma, twice as likely to earn a college degree, and most likely able to obtain a full-time working position by age 25. This research further detailed how SEL instruction leads students to having less emotional distress, fewer disciplinary incidents, increased school attendance, improved test scores, and higher grades (Frey, Fisher, & Smith, 2019; Mahoney, Durlak, & Weissberg, 2018).

Parents must recognize that their children are not born with the skills essential to manage emotions, solve problems, and get along with others. As already noted, too many parents cannot teach these skills because the parents themselves do not possess said skills. Therefore, the burden of responsibility lies on principals and teachers. This burden is no longer up for argument. The burden of responsibility is actually at a point of "do or lose"!

SEL skills must be taught in the school setting for the purpose of developing essential life skills. Otherwise, these skills—in the lives of too many children—will never be gained. Teaching SEL in schools is a win-win-win-win-win proposition: Teachers win. Principals win. Parents win. Students win. Society wins!

THREE IMPORTANT KEYS TO SEL IMPLEMENTATION

Principal Action #3: Embrace Social and Emotional Learning requires a shift in emphasis from the decades-old prescriptive testing and accountability standards to a broader definition of student success—notably the recognition that the development of crucial life skills in students goes hand in hand with academics and student achievement. Multiple keys to SEL implementation range from working in teams, to developing a culture of kindness and appreciation, to managing conflict with peer mediation, to specific teachings of social-emotional skills, to student voice in curricular and instructional decision-making, to self-monitoring, to reflective thinking and writing time, to creative thought and expression. However, for the purpose of this read, a vital focus is on three important keys to successful SEL implementation: 1) the establishment of routines (at school and at home); 2) the establishment of expectations (again, at school and at home); and 3) the establishment of research-based, student-centered, and best-practice SEL learning activities and teaching strategies.

Establish Routines

Students thrive in a setting of established routines and structures. Principals and teachers who create sound and specific routines and procedures for students to follow each school day immediately lower student anxiety and uneasiness and improve behaviors. The same is true in the home setting. Principals and teachers, for the emotional, social, and behavioral well-being of students, must stress, if not train, parents in very specific child-developmental routines to be observed in the home setting. School and home, working together, can only enhance the social and emotional well-being of children (at any age).

Establish Expectations

Principals set the standard when it comes to establishing expectations. Noted below is a six-step process for principals to ensure that clear SEL expectations are set.

1. *Reflect culture norms.* As expectations are adopted and/or revised, principals and team members must ensure that the expectations are reflective of surrounding community cultural values and norms.
2. *Recognize where expectations are required.* Principals need to ask questions such as, "Do expectation gaps for required behaviors exist?" and "How will the expectations affect student social and emotional behavior, campus culture, and/or the community culture?"
3. *Understand that everyone needs to realize the context, intention, and justification for the established expectations.* Students, teachers, and parents must know and understand the "why" as related to the establishment of any expectation.
4. *Meet and discuss with all parties the reason for the expectations and ensure that said expectations are recognized and understood.* Collaboration is a key factor. Principals must take time to meet with members of the learning community when establishing expectations.
5. *Provide for clarity of expectations by placing them in writing.* Remember, without written documentation (a student handbook, for example), rules don't exist.
6. *Enforce all expectations.* Enforcing expectations means clearly delineating and defining acceptable behaviors and then applying associated consequences. Desired behaviors and associated expectations are a principal's responsibility and must be an accepted norm for all students in every school. Student expectations include being respectful, responsible, and dependable. They must also be equal, equitable, and empathetically administered.

Establish Social and Emotional Learning Activities

Embracing, establishing, and teaching social and emotional skills is an absolute if students are to be successful at school, at home, in society, and in the future workplace. These skills build confidence, develop strengths, enhance weaknesses, allow for greater collaboration, aid in navigating social situations, develop stronger relationships, and permit students to make better decisions. SEL and associated skills are critical for all learners, at any age and any level of schooling.

Therefore, time must be designated for SEL activities and teaching strategies. Such must be identified and incorporated as schooling is expected to meet the needs of all students. Textbox 3.1. Examples of Social and Emotional Learning Activities at the Elementary Level and Textbox 3.2. Examples of Social and Emotional Learning Activities at the Secondary Level serve as guides for principals when leading, training, and coaching teachers in developing SEL pathways. Examine the SEL activities in Textboxes 3.1 and 3.2 and utilize these examples as guides when working with teachers.

SEVEN ESSENTIAL ATTRIBUTES OF SOCIAL AND EMOTIONAL LEARNING

Specific attributes or qualities, characteristics, and/or traits as associated with SEL as identified by CASEL (2020) are essential to the overall growth and development of young people who are expected to mature and become emotionally secure and socially sound as active students, adult citizens, and future leaders.

1. *Self-Awareness.* Students, to grow and develop socially and emotionally, must understand and exhibit emotions that influence positive personal behavior.
2. *Self-Maintenance.* Students must possess an ability to regulate their personal and public emotions and social behaviors. Associated personal and social/emotional proficiencies include self-monitoring and regulation, management of stressors, self-discipline, and overall management of decision-making and problem-solving functions.
3. *Social Awareness.* Students who assume a perspective of equality, equity, and empathy toward others are likely to develop into respectful and insightful adults. Related proficiencies include understanding; compassion; responsiveness; appreciation of individual and collective differences; and a genuine deference, consideration, and honorableness toward others.

TEXTBOX 3.1. EXAMPLES OF SOCIAL AND EMOTIONAL LEARNING ACTIVITIES AT THE ELEMENTARY LEVEL

Principals must lead teachers when it comes to integrating SEL activities and teaching strategies. Identified below are a few examples which principals can use to coach elementary teachers as a means of incorporating SEL activities.

Elementary School SEL Examples: Incorporate

Journal Writing (self-management)	Journal writing provides students an opportunity to consider and respond to questions such as "Identify a time when you curbed or controlled your emotions to help others." Students can then share their written responses with others in class.
Read Alouds (self-awareness)	While reading out loud, teachers can stop and take an opportunity to ask students how they believe the story character(s) think or feel and how they, as students, think or feel about the situation within the story.
Daily Greetings (relationship-building)	Begin the day with a positive social and emotional greeting such as showing a heart with hands, an air fist bump, a high-five, or a "send-a-hug" gesture. Give a thumbs-up or a simple "Hello, how are you today?"
Class Meetings (social awareness)	Hold a "morning" meeting each day or once a week. Use this meeting time to give students a voice—a chance to be heard whereby they can boost each other and help solve problems. Community space time promotes an open culture and positive classroom climate. Here's a starter question: "What qualities do you look for in a friend?" or "What are some positive friendship qualities you have?"
Responsibilities (responsibility orientation and self-management)	Provide students with certain classroom responsibilities (jobs such as class librarian, clean-up crew leader, etc.) to build a sense of self-worth, importance, and a recognition that work is meaningful and good for an individual.

This listing is but a small sample of SEL activities available to elementary school principals when guiding and coaching teachers. Other examples, to name a few, could include problem-solving and decision-making skill development activities, teamwork undertakings, diversity endeavors, kindness and empathy actions, coping skills measures, and respectfully disagreeing role-playing.

TEXTBOX 3.2. EXAMPLES OF SOCIAL AND EMOTIONAL LEARNING ACTIVITIES AT THE SECONDARY LEVEL

Principals must lead teachers when it comes to integrating SEL activities and teaching strategies. Identified below, are a few examples which principals can use to coach secondary teachers as a means of incorporating SEL activities.

Secondary School SEL Examples: Incorporate

Self-Awareness (How students focus on themselves when attempting to calm their reactions to certain circumstances)	Lead a class vocabulary activity by which students identify feelings they might have in differing situations. Ask, for example, "How would you feel if you got all As on your report card?" or "How would you feel if someone suggested on social media something ugly or disrespectful about your girlfriend or boyfriend?"
Self-Management (How students manage certain social and emotional circumstances or situations)	Utilizing a literature selection, ask students to identify a time they may have had the same feelings of the character(s) and how they were able to manage or handle themselves. Ask the students to discuss the question among themselves in small groups or have the students write a short essay in their journals.
Social Awareness (How perspective is an essential skill in written and spoken communication)	Define and discuss the term *empathy* and then teach a lesson relative to how to act, react, and communicate effectively. Include a discussion as to why it is important to properly respond to others and their feelings.

Responsible Decision-Making (How students have the ability to evaluate options and solve problems by making effective decisions)	Describe and discuss terms such as *responsibility, dependability, ethics, values, morality, honesty, equity,* and *equality*. Ask how these terms relate to being a good citizen, or community and family member, and how such relate to making proper decisions and solving problems.

This listing is but a small sample of SEL activities available to secondary school principals when guiding or coaching teachers. Other examples, to name a few, could include identity development, peer mentoring, establishing relationships, respectfulness, diversity, empathy, and teamwork.

4. *Social Management.* Students who maintain a positive self-image in social settings are able to recognize and regulate personal emotions, develop empathy for others; understand the significance of equitable and equal social relationships; build positive social, personal, and professional relationships; make responsible decisions; work effectively as a team member or leader; and handle, constructively, both socially and emotionally challenging situations and circumstances.
5. *Relationship Development.* Students possessing the ability to establish and maintain healthy and meaningful social and emotional relationships can expect to grow into more than social butterflies. Relationship development is all about focusing on achieving loyalties with friends, colleagues, and family members, and, ultimately, enhancing career interactions and opportunities.
6. *Responsible Decision-Making.* Students who reveal an ability to make proper and positive choices and who can further take responsibility for their personal actions, and learn from both positive and negative outcomes, are more likely to develop into socially and emotionally mature individuals.
7. *Reflective Problem-Solving.* According to Osterman and Kottkamp (2004) and York-Barr, Sommers, Ghere, and Monthie (2005), reflective problem-solving relates to students using social and emotional judgment to solve complex issues based on personal and previously gained knowledge and familiarity.

THE SOCIAL-EMOTIONAL LEARNING AND WELL-BEING CORRELATION

Research clarifies and supports Principal Action #3: Embrace Social and Emotional Learning with student well-being and long-term success (Jackson, Easton, Kiguel, Porter, & Blanchard, 2020). Key findings reveal several indices.

Students, notably at the high school level, who have engaged in SEL are more confident and skilled in the following areas: 1) interpersonal skills; 2) school connectedness (feeling a real part of the school and schooling); 3) academic efforts; 4) grit and determination; 5) academic engagement and achievement; 6) well-being and critical thinking and evaluative skills; 7) in- and out-of-school work habits; 8) long-term impacts (more likely to enroll in a four-year university as the SEL valued-added measures are stronger predictors of individual life success than test scores); 9) understanding of cultural differences; and 10) behaviors that are reflective of more civil, fair, equitable, equal, and empathetic attitudes toward others.

CONCLUDING COMMENTS

Today, a crisis in civility exists. SEL can bridge the gap between what is often termed offensive, disrespectful, discourteous, and/or boorish public behaviors and proper civility in communal discourse. Just think about the public ugliness displayed most recently in school board meetings across this nation. Moreover, a crisis in civics education exists as well. Over the last half century, civics education has all but been abandoned by many school systems. Teaching good citizenship, once a mainstay of public education, has been frequently sidelined by a focus on science, technology, mathematics, and high-stakes testing and accountability measures.

To that end, important subjects such as history and government and civics instruction have been forced to the educational back burner. The sidelining of civics and government, in particular, has contributed to America's incredibly low knowledge level of civic responsibilities, a failure to understand the three branches of government and their system of checks and balances, a lower voting rate, and a lack of appreciation for the fragility and vulnerability of democracy (Korbey, 2021).

As a result, a comeback of civics must be mandated, and the teaching of civics must include a heavy dose of SEL—the umbrella term for the development of non-academic skills such as managing emotions, advancing healthy interpersonal attitudes and perspectives, developing co-existing relationships, and fostering a more reasonable and responsible civic discourse (civility).

Each of these skills is designed to produce a more knowledgeable, thoughtful, and thoroughly engaged populace.

Principals must be leaders within and across the entire learning community when it comes to educating a new generation of considerate, respectful, well-informed, and civic-minded students. These students are our future citizenry, and they deserve to understand how a democracy works—for the benefit of all peoples!

FINAL THOUGHTS

Today, principals must understand the definition of SEL and how Principal Action #3: Embrace Social and Emotional Learning, as an educational process, relates to the well-being of students. Principals regularly appreciate and agree with the SEL precepts but frequently struggle to effectively incorporate SEL into instructional programming because of time constraints; funding issues; insufficient skill and values reinforcement at home; lack of teacher commitment, if not complete resistance; and parents who oppose schooling that incorporates values instruction.

Exceptional principals, however, recognize a solution to the above-noted inhibitors exists by means of a seven-step explanatory process: 1) strong and effective principal leadership, 2) dedicated funding, 3) SEL-oriented state accountability standards, 4) additional and positive SEL effects research, 5) increased training and professional development, 6) district curricular and instructional support for SEL implementation, and 7) the development of SEL student assessment instruments as part of teacher evaluative measures.

Exceptional principals understand, profess, and embrace the importance of SEL and share with teachers, students, and parents the numerous benefits of SEL. These benefits, further exemplified in Chapter 4, include student self-awareness, self-maintenance, social awareness, social management, relationship development, responsible decision-making, and reflective problem-solving. These principals also acknowledge and incorporate two keys to successful SEL implementation: 1) the establishment of routines at school and, just as important, at home; and 2) the establishment of student, teacher, and parent expectations.

DISCUSSION QUESTIONS

1. While it is obvious that Principal Action #3: Embrace Social and Emotional Learning is important in the school setting, principals all too often regularly appreciate yet struggle with initiation and implementation of the SEL instructional process. Examine the seven explanatory

solutions, as listed earlier in the chapter. Identify three that you believe are critical to SEL success in schools. Be detailed in your response, explaining why.
2. Consider the chapter section entitled "SEL and Its Importance to Teachers, Students, and Parents." Identify a common thread tying all three entities together. Clarify why the identified thread is a critically important aspect of SEL.
3. Reflect upon the chapter section entitled "Three Important Keys to SEL Implementation." Why are establishing routines and expectations essential to the embracing and implementing of SEL?
4. Within the chapter section "Establish Expectations," a six-step process is detailed. Which one of the six steps is most central to embracing and implementing SEL in schools? Expound.
5. Within the chapter is a detailed analysis of seven essential attributes of SEL. Examine each of the seven attributes and explain which one of the seven attributes could best aid and support the students you personally serve. Why and by what means?

CASE STUDY APPLICATION: GETTING BACK TO THE BUSINESS OF SCHOOLING FOLLOWING MUCH DISORDER: A PRINCIPAL LEARNS HOW TO LEAD A SOCIALLY RESPONSIVE, EMOTIONALLY SAFE, AND MORE PREDICTABLE LEARNING ENVIRONMENT

"Now this! What's next?" A statement and a query voiced by Assistant Principal Cinnamon Carter. It had been a most difficult week. The light at the end of the tunnel had yet to be reached, let alone seen. Time was on the side of the students and teachers and administrative team, but time was ever fleeting. Yes, it had been a most difficult week. Much work lay ahead.

Students and faculty had previously experienced the emotional trauma of the public health crisis, with far too many losing loved ones to the pandemic. However, the general public and the students at Rollin Landau School were slowly but surely overcoming the ill-fated aspects of the deadly virus. Life had just begun to return to some level of normalcy—if life could ever be described as normal. The entire "return-to-school" process had initially been a "mission impossible," but with solid teamwork, administrative leadership, and wise, student-centered, health-science-orientated decision-making, students and faculty were now safe and striving to advance and achieve.

"Now this," Assistant Principal Carter said again. Principal Jim Phelps sat at his desk, using the index and middle fingers of his hands to slowly rub his temples. He remained in deep thought, not responding to his assistant principal's statement or query. The father of one of his students had been the victim of a brutal beating by sources not yet validated. The father was clinging to life, but just barely. An older sister of another one of the school's students had also been brutally beaten and died in transport to a local hospital. As a result of the violence, the community had erupted into protests, some peaceful, others more violent with looting and other malicious misbehaviors occurring. Tolerance was fading fast. Equitable, equal, and empathetic community actions and treatments were in short supply.

Certain community leaders believed the beatings and the one death were both at the hands of local supremacists. Others blamed the police department for not responding quickly enough to disrupt and arrest the agitators. It was a community in chaos and the turmoil had bled over into the school setting. Students were visibly upset, if not in a high state of agitation. The same could be said of most of the school's teachers and staff members. Moments earlier, teacher Barney Collier had stormed into the office and shouted, "We need to stage a school-wide walkout! Enough is enough. I'm sick and tired of what is happening in our community and school. I'm encouraging both teachers and students to walk out! Do you hear me?" Mr. Collier had quickly turned around, slammed the office door, and left. Disturbed and tormented, Principal Phelps stood up from behind his desk and walked toward the assistant principal. The principal's face was grim but now more determined than ever.

Principal Jim Phelps said, "Cinnamon, things are really getting out of control, and we have to positively influence the situation. It goes without saying that our students are in desperate need of feeling safe, secure, and supported equally and empathetically, especially here at school. They require a more encouraging, equitable, and accommodating learning environment as well as stronger teacher/student relationships because emotional, social, and academic learning is at a fragile state and must be optimized. Our students have experienced way too much trauma, been exposed to more than their fair share of unpredictable events, continue to experience emotionally draining supervision at home, and possess real insecurities. You and I both know that a negative displacement has engulfed our school and our community. We must restore the well-being of our students, faculty, and parents to a higher level of social-civil discourse and emotional normalcy. What has happened is tragic, and we must do even better by our students. Our students need us, now!" At that time, the two campus counselors, Willi Armitage and Dana Briggs, stepped into the principal's office.

Principal Phelps and his assistant principal, Cinnamon Carter, looked at one another and then at the counselors. Willi Armitage stared back and said, "I see it in your eyes. You need our help. More important, you need answers!" Willi then turned to Dana Briggs and said, "Okay, Dana, we've arrived just in time. Let's share our plan of action!"

Principals, assistant principals, and faculties in schools across America frequently find themselves in the depths of social and emotional stress, if not distress. They require help, they need answers, and they deserve a plan of action to bring aid to their students. As a basis for establishing a plan of action, consider the following:

Lewis, Mitchell, Horner, and Sugai (2017) and McIntosh et al. (2020), in studies regarding building partnerships with multi-tiered systems of support, recommend six strategies for principals and school teams to ensure a school positively and effectively addresses the social and emotional well-being and needs of students. Schools must provide a safe, caring, and predictable learning environment, particularly after a major disruptive event. Mungal and Sorenson (2020) recommend two additional strategies. All eight strategies are identified below:

- *Remind, reteach, and acknowledge the effectiveness of SEL as a school-wide instructional program and expectation.* A strong focus on reminding students, often by reteaching, of specified SEL expectations—through modeling established and desired school and classroom behaviors—is important. Doing so aids in reestablishing and maintaining an open school culture whereby students can expect to observe routines and actions that are prosocial, fair, equitable, equal, and most empathetic.
- *Reexamine classroom activities.* Principals and teachers must establish a supportive learning community and emphasize positive and proactive campus and classroom support, approaches, and activities. Note the following examples:
  - Establish a conducive physical classroom setting with predictable routines and SEL expectations.
  - Actively supervise students by providing high rates of interactions with and from all students, always positively acknowledging students with praise and recognition, and providing prompts and pre-corrections before a misbehavior can occur.
  - Proactively utilize social and emotional teaching and learning strategies to reward resulting and appropriate behaviors and thus create optimal instructional time and settings.
- *Focus on the social and emotional well-being of all students.* As previously examined in Chapter 1, the social and emotional well-being of students is strongly correlated with structure and predictability in teaching and learning (Mungal & Sorenson, 2020). Beachboard (2020) reminds principals and teachers to focus on student well-being at all times but especially during times of difficulty, disruptions, and crises.

Beachboard asserts that this focus must be through an ongoing process of support that is correlated with the 3Cs: *communication, consistency,* and *control. Communication* is all about a mental health or emotional well-being check-in process. Checking in with students and allowing them to talk about their problems and vent their frustrations and negative emotions with someone they trust (frequently a teacher) is profoundly healing and reduces stress, strengthens resolve, and diminishes periods of distress (refer back to the *Do We Really Matter?* case study in Chapter 1, as an example).

Consistency is a key to emotional and social well-being during difficult and changing times. Consistency must be as close to a norm as possible both in the classroom and at home. One "at-home" example that principals can work with teachers in developing is providing families with a sample schedule.

Control provides students with a sense of controlling their own lives—socially and emotionally, especially when they are completely consumed with anxiety, anger, fear, or apprehension. Control, as detailed by Beachboard (2020), includes the following:

- Student identification of support structures such as people or activities that help students to feel better. Support structures are identified as those individuals to whom students can turn in times of social and emotional need.
- A listing of stressors that are "speed bumps" or "detours"—if not "stop signs" or "red lights" that inhibit social and emotional well-being. Identifying and acknowledging specific personal stressors enables students to create support options or tools to best address the identified barriers.
- *Avoid punitive approaches to managing students following a disruptive social or emotional event.* Students who have experienced trauma require understanding, empathy, and acknowledgment. Punitive behavioral approaches during a period of trauma actually inflict more trauma. Avoid such practices. Talk with misbehaving students about their inappropriate behaviors, the reason(s) for said behaviors, and, just as important, those appropriate behaviors which should be exhibited.
- *Positively and personally meet, greet, and interact with all students.* Simple actions such as the daily greeting of students must be a principal norm (Mungal & Sorenson, 2020). Such is the basis for placing students at ease, enhancing student-principal engagement, and, furthermore, identifying those students in need of social and emotional support.
- *Carefully look for signs when students need emotional and social help.* Students in need frequently exhibit signs such as isolation, dependency, moodiness, apathy, victimization, excessive absences, self-abuse,

disciplinary issues, fits of anger, truancy, poor academic performance, conflict with adults, noncompliance, and/or aggressiveness (Gresham, MacMillan, & Bocian, 1996). Additionally, student posts on social media, while often ignored, must be perceived as potential postings of cries for help.

- *Reconnect with students.* Make every attempt to value the individual strengths of students, noting and responding to their individual differences, skills, and personalities. For students who have experienced extreme personal loss, it is essential to allow for bonding, to understand and empathize with their recent traumatic experiences, and to allow these students an opportunity to have a voice: to talk, vent, and/or share (Mungal & Sorenson, 2020).
- *Reengage families as school partners.* Establishing common ground between school and home, specifically as related to safety, trauma, disruptions, and responsibilities, can be a source of comfort to a student and their family members. Principals and teams must be recognized as sources of community support and unity whereby families can reach out in times of need.

APPLICATION QUESTIONS

1. How could Principal Action #3: Embrace Social and Emotional Learning best assist Principal Jim Phelps and his team relative to the well-being of the students at Rollin Landau School? Provide supportive evidence based on the chapter readings.
2. The Rollin Landau School counselors, Willi Armitage and Dana Briggs, bring a plan of action to the school's leadership team. The plan, based on research studies, identifies eight strategies to better ensure that the SEL and well-being of students occurs, particularly following a major disruptive event. Reexamine each of the eight strategies. Which four of the eight strategies do you perceive would be best suited to meet the social and emotional needs of the Rollin Landau School students? Explain your reasoning.
3. Beachboard (2020), as noted in the *Focus on the Social and Emotional Well-Being of All Students* segment, recommends principals and teams initiate the 3Cs: communication, consistency, and control. Which of these 3Cs could best benefit students at Rollin Landau School? Be detailed in your explanation.
4. Within the chapter section "Establish Expectations," there is a six-step process for principals to ensure that clear SEL expectations are set.

Which three of the six steps best apply or relate to the principal, faculty, and students at Rollin Landau School? Which one(s) does not?
5. How could the students at Rollin Landau School benefit from the seven essential attributes of social and emotional learning identified in the chapter? Be specific in your explanation.
6. Teacher Barney Collier, in the case study, asserts the following: "We need to stage a school-wide walkout! Enough is enough. I'm sick and tired of what is happening in our community and school. I'm encouraging both teachers and students to walk out! Do you hear me?" What does your school district policy stipulate relative to the statement and proposed action of Mr. Collier? How would you, as a principal, handle this personnel issue? What guidelines does your district personnel policy offer? Why is it important, for the well-being of students and faculty, to follow school district/board policy? What social and emotional well-being considerations as identified in Chapters 1 and 2 might apply as a means to aid and support Mr. Collier?
7. Explain why Principal Action #3: Embrace Social and Emotional Learning is considered an important topic and process in education and for what good reasons.

Chapter 4

Principal Action #4
Appreciate Social and Emotional Learning

WELCOME THE BENEFITS, RECOGNIZE THE CHALLENGES

"Principals can improve the social and emotional development of their students, even as early as preschool!"—Lloyd Goldsmith, former principal and professor emeritus

THE BENEFITS OF SOCIAL AND EMOTIONAL LEARNING

SEL readily correlates with student achievement. Studies conducted by the Collaborative for Academic, Social, and Emotional Learning (2011); the AEI Brookings Working Group on Poverty and Opportunity(2015); Durlak, Weissberg, Dymnicki, Taylor, and Schellinger (2011); Princeton-Brookings (2017); and the Wallace Foundation (2021) all found students who participate in SEL score significantly higher academically, maintain higher graduation rates, and are more likely to graduate from college.

Principal Action #4: Appreciate Social and Emotional Learning relates to what the research attests: ninety-eight percent of school principals surveyed acknowledged that students benefit from being taught social and emotional skills (Jones et al., 2017). Identified below are seven benefits of SEL.

Benefit #1: Cultural Responsiveness Creates Five Essential Schooling Components

1. *Identity and Identity Awareness.* A student's identity is made up of race and ethnicity, culture, gender identity, language, religion, sexual identity, and socioeconomic status—all of which influence a student's social and emotional experiences. Principals and faculties must exercise what is known as identity awareness (a consciousness of various critical identities). Identity can positively or negatively influence students and their ability to learn, achieve, socialize, behave, and construct an overall social and emotional well-being.

    Principals and faculty must also recognize their own personal identities and how these identities impact teaching, leading, and learning. Furthermore, principals and faculty must understand and appreciate the identity of their students' families and community members, and just as important, the identity of the school (whether it be good or not so good).

    Identity awareness provides perspectives and enhances knowledge and understanding about the students, their families, and the community in which the students reside. Identity awareness can also reveal much about a school both in terms of climate and culture. It is critical that principals and team members engage all students and stakeholders without assuming one set of experiences is representative of all individuals.

    Identity awareness is all about educators overcoming the simplistic notion that one's personal identity is the identity of every student and parent. People are different. They come from different backgrounds, cultures, experiences, and opportunities (or lack thereof). Therefore, all peoples (students, parents, and community members) must be understood, respected, and appreciated for who they are, what they do, and how they respond to the process called schooling.

2. *Voice.* As noted in Chapter 1, the well-being of a learning community relates to voice—the ability to verbally engage and be heard. Voice is more than verbalizing thoughts. Voice requires students, teachers, parents, and community members to become active participants and exercise leadership within schools. Voice is all about active engagement in school-related areas such as:
    - parental involvement
    - community members providing knowledge, input, guidance, and expertise
    - students participating in curricular and instructional decision-making
    - eliciting cultural values, especially those of underrepresented students and families

- stakeholder partnerships from those families beyond the Black and Latinx cultures, for example, African nation populations: Somalian, Kenyan, Ethiopian, Nigerian, Ugandan, Tanzanian, etc.; or Native American populations: Oneida, Huron, Wyandot, Lakota, Pima, Mescalero Apache, etc.

These students and their families often remain in the shadows. Their partnerships require school principals and teams to move beyond identifying communities from a racial perspective to recognizing and giving voice to the cultures and ethnicities they serve.

3. *Supportive Environment*. Principal Action #4: Appreciate Social and Emotional Learning is all about developing a supportive instructional environment all for the well-being of students. A supportive environment is one in which an open culture and positive climate is the norm and where encouragement, rather than a system of infractions, is fostered and fortified as a measure of developing desired social and emotional behaviors.

A supportive environment is one in which the principal and faculty understand how essential it is to hold one another accountable when working toward the social and emotional well-being of all members of the learning community. Principal and faculty must understand the obligation of meeting the needs of all students by addressing the critical development of essential SEL skills, as well as improving and enhancing student behaviors, especially when there is a cultural mismatch. Punishing students into assimilation is a terrible wrong.

Within a supportive environment, students, parents, and community members feel socially and emotionally valued and are encouraged to share aspects of their culture and history as opposed to learning about the dominant culture and history. Diversity is welcomed and, moreover, incorporated into classroom lessons, hallway displays, school programs, and overall instructional programming.

4. *Situational Appropriateness*. Situational appropriateness is all about a principal and faculty determining the types of social and emotional behaviors that will safeguard positive student-oriented outcomes, all the while ensuring students demonstrate the best behavioral skills and attributes.

Typically, situational appropriateness relates to students and faculty with both groups explicitly learning legitimate social and emotional behaviors that are viewed as appropriate in a student's home or community setting and culture and in the school setting. As a result, behavior instruction at school must be tailored to the context or situation in which the behavior occurs.

Bastable, Fairbanks Falcon, Nese, Meng, and McIntosh (2019) note that the Center on Positive Behavioral Interventions and Supports calls this process "code-switching"—a means by which a type of behavior that is exhibited by students in a classroom and deemed unacceptable could very well be the same type of behavior modeled in the presence of friends and is recognized as being completely acceptable and situationally appropriate. Students recognizing, knowing, and incorporating the "when", "how", and "why" aspects of following certain behavioral expectations find it critically important to optimize behaviors that are situationally appropriate, socially acceptable, and civility-tolerant.

To ensure such a connection and, thus, to incorporate it within teaching, leading, and learning processes, principals and teachers must examine student definitions of acceptable behaviors at home, with friends, and in the community at large, and then share the commonalities and differences when compared with school behavioral expectations.

At this point, Principal Action #4: Appreciate Social and Emotional Learning must be targeted to said commonalities and differences with student attention tied to recognizing and accepting the dynamics of the culturally accepted norms and differences at school and in the classroom when compared with those of the cultural/environmental norms of home, community, and friends.

Example: The common use, by students and many millennials in general, of the "F-word" or "F-bomb" is frequently an accepted public practice. In most school settings, if not many social environments, this word is unacceptable but too often tolerated. So as not to be perceived as prudish or preachy, many would stipulate there is a time and place, if at all, for such talk.

To overlap this communication style with that of the "outside-the-school" setting and that of the culturally accepted norms within a school, students using the F-word (especially when they are excited or confused or believe the term makes or serves as a meaningful contribution to a conversation) might find it hard to believe that using such a term is in actuality viewed by many as one which is disruptive, interruptive, insulting, and disrespectful, and should, therefore, be corrected with disciplinary action. The teaching of socially and emotionally acceptable language is a must in schools today.

Situational Appropriateness Resolution: When one student, during a passing period or even in the classroom, says to another student, "Go F-yourself" in seriousness or jest, and at the same time, the student happens to be overheard by a teacher or a couple of teachers, it is time for a situational appropriateness resolution.

The situationally appropriate and/or culturally responsive model approach would be for the teacher(s) to stop the student and aid the student in understanding that the use of the communicative tool—from outside to inside the school learning environment—is not only inappropriate but insensitive on the part of the student.

Explaining that while the female teachers have previously in life heard the F-word, and possibly even used the same term privately, it is by no means, within the school setting, a verbally useful, publicly acceptable, or culturally responsive term of use.

If as a principal or educator you are thinking, "This is so familiar," well, you are right. Situational appropriateness is as old as the ages. It is nothing more than a principal or teacher or community member or any other adult simply instructing a young person, giving advice or guidance as your own parent or teacher of years ago did. Could a student respond with an "F-you"? Possibly so. However, a lesson in SEL has been taught, explained, and done so with limited recrimination.

Time for Reflection: Principals who fail to lead, coach, guide, model, and/or instruct their students in what is situationally appropriate are, at the very least, failing to serve. Recall a time when your own mother or father, or an aunt or uncle, or that special grandmother or grandfather pulled you aside and said to you, either privately or quite publicly, "What you just said [or did] was not appropriate!"

Then and there, you were informed, guided, directed, or simply taught, with love and positive emotion, the difference between what is right and what is wrong. Now, think for a moment: The lesson worked, did it not? Students, today, require the same treatment—treatment that is based on the emotions of love, fairness, firmness, and respectfulness (Einhorn, 2022). Give them their due!

5. *Data for Student Equity.* Principals and faculties who incorporate Principal Action #4: Appreciate Social and Emotional Learning must be culturally responsive, specifically by disaggregating and analyzing data to plan for instructional improvements, and to collaborate regarding data trends and potential solutions notably as related to equity, equality, race, and culture. Principals and instructional teams must always focus on positive change and always refrain from passing judgments on students, parents, and each other.

Principals and instructional planning teams must incorporate two different types of data: 1) student outcome data and analyses, and 2) fidelity (reliability or trustworthiness) of implementation data and analyses. As campus leadership and team members analyze data, the impact of disparities will become apparent. "Business as usual" can no longer serve as a model for curricular and instructional development and incorporation.

The American education system, principals must understand, was designed by a dominant ethnicity. Student populations, today, in many respects are no longer defined by this dominant group. Thus, subgroups can be adversely affected. Failure will then become a norm as related to academics, behaviors, and SEL and responses.

Example: A principal and campus improvement planning team note that an unusually high number of disciplinary referrals has occurred over time. Data analyses reveals this problem. The "who" and "why" questions must be posed. The "who" in this example are Latinx students (more specifically, the growing on-campus El Salvadorian population). Principal Action #4: Appreciate Social and Emotional Learning is a critical link to best ensuring the utilization of data for purposes of equity and equality. Principal and team members decide to:

- Confirm that culturally authentic and responsive professional development addresses the growing student population, notably from the perspective of SEL and, more specifically, from an understanding of and respect for the El Salvadorian culture.
- Instruct students and their parents as to what critical skills are required to enhance academic performance as well as student behavior. Detail the purpose of said skills and behaviors.
- Define "non-compliance" and its application at school to the El Salvadorian students. Explain to their parents as well.

Time for Reflection: Student equity, equality, and understanding requires a principal and faculty to seek information about the Salvadorian students (as described in the example), their families, and community leaders. Learn the language of the students and their families and recognize and appreciate the cultural norms of their community. Then, engage all parties with an emphasis on compassion, understanding, equity, and equality. This is the beginning of a culturally responsive and socially emotionally instructive process and experience that brings about improved relations when it comes to the students, their families, and their community.

Benefit #2: Critical Thinking Is Enhanced

Principal Action #4: Appreciate Social and Emotional Learning Social is designed to aid students in better understanding how to think, critically, and learn what is essential to thrive—not only in school but in society. Self-reflection, as a critical thinking skill, is targeted. Self-reflection serves as a means by which students can neutrally examine their thoughts, feelings, emotions, and actions. Through this practice, students are able to look at themselves with a deeper level or critical degree of interest, curiosity, and philosophy of self.

SEL further aids learners in developing much needed problem-solving skills in all areas of life. This helps students focus on managing situations in life, as well as problems in school or academics or with interpersonal skill development. Thus, SEL guides students in understanding consequences; making choices based on priority, time, and social awareness; and how proper life and academic skill development impacts themselves as well as others. Coping skills reduce emotional distress and appropriately manage feelings, passions, sensations, and reactions.

Benefit #3: Academic Achievement Is Increased

Social and emotional skills readily correlate with improved academic performance. Such SEL skills which enhance learning and achievement include goal-setting, planning, organization, time management, problem-solving, decision-making, cooperating, collaborating, thought-organizing, and focusing techniques. As previously noted, student test scores improve as a result of SEL skill development. When students recognize that they are listened to and thus sense they are respected in their classrooms, they become more motivated, their attitudes improve, and ultimately students become much more confident in their abilities to learn and achieve.

Benefit #4: Student Behaviors Are Improved

Every principal and team dream of fewer student disciplinary issues. SEL provides much needed avenues for decreasing disciplinary incidents. All too often, behavior problems are the result of skill deficits. Improved student behaviors are often equated to an ability to problem solve, develop peer relationships, and manage emotions. Studies have provided positive insight relative to students behaving better with each other (bullying subsides), their teachers, and their parents following engagement in SEL (Belfield et al., 2015; Jones et al., 2021).

Moreover, recent studies are indicative of SEL students having fewer psychological problems, anger disputes, and substance abuse issues (Duckworth et al., 2012; Espelage, Low, Polanin, & Brown, 2013; Montague, Enders, Cavendish, & Castro, 2011; Sklad, Diekstra, DeRitter, Ben, & Gravestein, 2012). When students are equipped with skills for managing their emotions, learn to practice self-control, build team collaborative efforts, and develop peer and teacher relationships (all taught as SEL skills), confidence in self and respect for others increase, and interpersonal conflict abates.

To this point within Chapter 4, evidence regarding SEL benefits has pointedly leaned toward student populations as sole beneficiaries. Let's now consider how SEL can readily and more purposefully aid principals and teachers.

Benefit #5: Data Analysis and Evaluation Are Expanded

Transforming any aspect of schooling requires advanced research, policy development, practice enhancement, teamwork, and strong and effective leadership, with efficient data analysis and programmatic evaluation. One of the essential benefits of Principal Action #4: Appreciate Social and Emotional Learning is principal recognition and understanding of data-based decision-making utilization, fidelity (reliable, trustworthy, and dependable) data incorporation, and data for equity (just and fair) application. First, more specific definitions of each data term:

1. *Data-based decision-making* or data-driven decision-making refers to principals and instructional teams engaging in an ongoing process of collecting and analyzing different types of data, including demographic information, student achievement test results, and satisfaction survey results, and then processing said data to best guide decisions relative to overall programmatic and organizational improvement.
2. *Fidelity data* and associated information and outcomes is typified as a direct reflection of how well the principal, leadership team members, and faculty data drivers are working in conjunction to support teachers and students, as both are users and recipients of educational interventions or innovations. Fidelity in data refers to how closely prescribed procedures are followed and, in the context of schooling, the degree to which principals and teachers implement programs, assessments, and curricular/instructional programmatic enhancements and changes according to reliable and trustworthy data-based methods.

    When interventions are implemented with fidelity, principals and teachers are able to make more accurate and fair decisions about a student's progress and future interventional needs. In addition, fidelity of implementation to the data-based individualization process helps to ensure that principals and instructional teams have essential resources and curricular processes in place to support effective, if not essential, instructional implementations for both individual students and broad student groups across campus.
3. *Data for equity* is identified as a process through which schools, led by principals, build their capacity for using data to make significant strategic, yet just, decisions and programmatic changes. This data type

is analyzed through an equity lens by examining the methods by which data is collected, interpreted, and disseminated.

Data for equity underscores student marginalization from the perspective of how unequal opportunities to access can be incorporated, and how the misuse of unfair or unjust data can and will harm students. This form of data analyses raises the issue of data sovereignty, and the democratization of data. Data for equity pushes principals to consider how the mis-practice of data analysis can reinforce stereotypes and exacerbate problems such as racial bias or further undermine social justice.

Next, it is critical for principals to acknowledge, if not value, that varying types of data analysis can provide relevant snapshots of what students are learning or, just as important, are not learning, and how instructional or programmatic adjustments can be incorporated to better meet student academic needs. Appropriate analysis and interpretation of data permits principals and teachers to make informed decisions which will positively affect student outcomes.

SEL data collection from differing data types provides for real-time recordings of student behaviors and social-emotional skills development and definitely serves as a tool for effective identification of instructional baselines, the establishment of realistic curricular goals and teaching objectives, and, thus, the successful monitoring of teaching adjustments and student academic progress. Data-based decision-making utilization, fidelity data incorporation, and data for equity application ultimately provide a principal the opportunity to measure SEL effectiveness, to direct informed instructional decisions, to make curricular adjustments, to guide and enhance teacher professional development, to scrutinize student achievement, to plan for future SEL implementation practices, to monitor and review leadership capacity, and to ultimately celebrate successes.

Benefit #6: Team Involvement Advances

Since Principal Action #4: Appreciate Social and Emotional Learning is a process of developing and utilizing social and emotional skills, coping with feelings, setting goals, making decisions, solving problems, getting along, and feeling empathy for others, teamwork is inherently a most positive by-product! Team involvement evolves around relationship development—the expansion, advancement, and overall improvement of communication, cooperation, and conflict resolution.

As a result, students (and guess what, teachers and leadership staff, too) learn how to work well with others. More collaborative efforts develop. Partnerships progress. Small-group interactions become a norm. Problem-solving, through difficult interactions or during disagreements, progresses. Becoming a good team player is a critically positive and successful result. Most important, natural leadership skills develop in both students and school community adults.

Benefit #7: Learning Gaps Diminish

Recent research is indicative of a continued increase in learning gaps, an increase that is both pervasive and profound. Dorn, Hancock, Sarakatsannis, and Viruleg (2021), in a report for the research firm and consulting institution McKinsey & Company, suggest that students, as a result of the recent health crisis, have lost anywhere from 3 to 12 months of learning. This significant depth of learning loss can be attributed to the following three factors:

1. The quality of remote learning.
2. The types of school support (technical, therapeutic, human, fiscal, material).
3. At-risk factors. Consider that special education students have the gravest risk of failure according to the Office for Civil Rights (2021). Additionally, students of color (Black, Latinx, and Asian) and low-income students are early victims of the recent increase in learning gaps.

Questions: What can mitigate these alarming factors? What can shrink the learning gap(s)? Answer: The immediate and active engagement of SEL.

The research is crystal clear regarding SEL as an effective intervention when seeking to help students catch up (Jones et al., 2021).

SEL researchers advocate five critical aspects of schooling (teaching, leading, and learning) which must be in place for students to advance and achieve academically: 1) in-person attendance and active student engagement, 2) appropriate grade-level/subject-area content, 3) core curriculum advancing SEL, 4) increased and uninterrupted teaching time which focuses on SEL, and 5) face-to-face teaching with a SEL focus (Linlin, Flynn, DeRosier, Weiser, & Austin-King 2021).

Each of these five essential schooling characteristics is not only correlated with Principal Action #4: Appreciate Social and Emotional Learning but with the diminishing of student achievement gaps. Principals who promote the teaching and development of strong social and emotional skills better ensure the academic performance of all students, especially those most at risk of failure. Research has consistently revealed that students who develop via SEL teaching and learning not only improve their attitudes toward their academic performance but also increase their achievement by 11 percentile points (Counseling Teacher, 2021; Options for Youth, 2021; Victoria State Government Education and Training, 2021).

One final note regarding the benefits of SEL. What improves within and across a school community? Campus and classroom culture and climate improves. Student motivation increases. Students learn to establish and exceed in goal development. Study habits improve. Mental health is enhanced. Empathy evolves. Self-regulation improves. Disagreeing becomes respectful. Self-awareness increases. Perseverance, resilience, and tenacity are highlighted. Confidence expands. Attendance improves. Equity and equality is enhanced. Furthermore, teachers cope better and develop an improved attitude regarding students and instruction, itself.

COMMON CHALLENGES WHEN IMPLEMENTING SEL IN SCHOOLS

Change brings challenges. Change brings resistance. The text *Responding to Resisters: Tactics That Work for Principals* (2021) relates that "the only change people truly like is that which jingles in their pocket" (p. 8). Most would agree. When implementing SEL in schools, principals must be aware of numerous challenges to bringing the curricular and instructional process to fruition. So, again, the question: "What's a principal to do?"

What Principals Must Know and Understand

First, recognize that uncertainty and disruption (even minimal) at the campus level can take a toll on all stakeholders: students, teachers, parents, and even principals. Programmatic or organizational changes can lead to stress for and resistance from teaching teams, negative climates and/or closed cultures, strained relationships, and what some at the campus level might consider irrelevant or unequitable teaching and learning experiences.

So, what must principals know and understand when it comes to implementing SEL and what are the common challenges? Identified below are seven potential distractors for principals to expect:

1. Resources (human, fiscal, and material) are absolutes to initiating a campus-wide SEL program.
2. Integration of another new or different instructional program requires patience, equipment, digital tools, community dialogue, and reexamination of traditional classroom teaching and learning by asking two simple

questions: "Is doing what we are doing still working? Is the program or process really effective?"

3. Proceed with caution, always! A Houston suburb principal recently asked, "Why should I rock the boat when the deep blue sea is so calm?" Good question, especially when that "deep blue sea" is a euphemism for "school"! Teachers need guidance when it comes to implementing any new process or program.

   Time is typically in short supply in schools, today. Patience can be as well. Principals must act wisely and recognize teacher burnout is often exasperated by lack of leader communication, appropriate professional development, critical information to guide instructional change, and resource allocation.

   While teachers across the nation believe, and research has consistently confirmed, SEL supports rather than detracts from academic learning, getting from Point A (Instructional Change) to Point B (Recognition of the Good) can be, at the very least, challenging. Principals must lead, guide, direct, and coach with careful consideration of others and always with caution!

4. A superintendent once told the author of this text, "It's all politics" (J. Thedford, personal communication, 1995). Today is supercharged with politics—national, state, local, and definitely school. Yet, principals must wade into the social justice pool and be prepared to promote equity and equality (see Chapter 5).

   Principals can readily rely on Principal Action #4: Appreciate Social and Emotional Learning and associated competencies and strategies to emphasize issues related to equity and equality by acknowledging and navigating the difficult aspects and conversations associated with power, privilege, race, bigotry, racism, prejudice, and other social justice issues. Challenging? Yes! Must a principal avoid the unavoidable? No!

5. Time is critical and essential to building relationships across the entire learning community. Such relationship development must include students, teachers, staff, parents, and community members. Forging connections, both formal and informal, takes time and requires dedicated efforts. Recall the old adage "Nothing is perfect. Challenges abound. Life is messy. Relationships are complex. Outcomes are uncertain. People can be irrational. But we desperately need one another!" Also, remember: The well-being of the learning community adults is an important precursor to the well-being and social and emotional development of the students!

6. Principals are challenged with crafting community agreement by sharing the reality of the moment, defining student-centered aims, and holding all parties accountable. Principals must also rise to the challenge of

crediting the capabilities of others; recognizing and celebrating progress, even when minimal; and always remaining nimble on their feet. Remember, expect the unexpected in the forms of community disagreement; teaching, leading, and learning design setbacks; and the all too often technical adaptations, adjustments, and malfunctions.
7. Principals must lead. Always a challenge but critical to the success of all parties. Why else do principals earn the big bucks? Right, you chuckle! The principalship has been described as a 10,000-aspirin job. So, how does a principal meet the challenge and not overdose on the aspirin? Consider the following:
   - Place a premium on principal leadership. Students must always come first!
   - Be a person of quality and integrity—act ethically, morally, and legally.
   - Engage instructionally and be academically focused.
   - Build a positive climate, open culture, and productive work environment.
   - Collaborate and facilitate in everything.
   - Manage personnel professionally and strategically.
   - Lead for equity and teach and preach equality.

FINAL THOUGHTS

Exceptional principals recognize the numerous benefits of incorporating Principal Action #4: Appreciate Social and Emotional Learning into a schooling's curriculum and instructional process. While the benefits are numerous, seven have been identified:
1. Cultural responsiveness creates essential schooling components such as identity and identity awareness, voice, supportive learning environments, situational appropriateness, and data essential for student equity.
2. Critical thinking is enhanced.
3. Academic achievement is increased.
4. Student behaviors are improved.
5. Data analysis and evaluation are expanded.
6. Team involvement advances.
7. Learning gaps diminish.

Exceptional principals also realize there will be common challenges associated with the implementation of SEL in schools. Such challenges include:

- Resources (human, fiscal, and material) and the lack thereof.

- Program integration, which requires patience, equipment, digital tools, community dialogue, and regular evaluation.
- Proceeding with caution—always. Principal communication efforts, appropriate professional development, critical information dissemination, and resource allocations will aid in overcoming the challenges to SEL implementation.
- Politics, politics, politics. Inequity and inequality and negativity—if not outright bigoted conversations regarding power, race, privilege, racism, prejudice, and social justice is always a detriment to any programmatic change and initiation.
- Relationship development is required to forge essential connections, but time continues to be an enemy.
- Agreement to make an instructional change within and across the learning community.
- Principal leadership. A premium to the effective implementation of SEL is principal leadership. Such will always be a challenge to organizational and instructional advancement if lacking or non-existent.

Exceptional principals who initiate and lead effectively with Principal Action #4: Appreciate Social and Emotional Learning are individuals of quality. They act ethically, morally, and legally. These leaders engage others instructionally and are always academically focused. They build a positive climate, open culture, and a productive work environment. Exceptional principals collaborate (I'm here to work with you) with others, always facilitating (I'm here to help you) throughout any change process. These principals manage personnel professionally and strategically and they always lead for equity and teach and preach equality.

DISCUSSION QUESTIONS

1. Research has consistently revealed that Principal Action #4: Appreciate Social and Emotional Learning benefits students, teachers, and principals. The initial chapter paragraph details several reasons for SEL correlating with student achievement. Identify those correlations and then conduct a digital engine search to identify three additional benefits of SEL.
2. Why is *voice* considered a student benefit of SEL? Explain.
3. Examples and times for reflection are within the chapter section entitled "Benefit 1" under item 4. Situational Appropriateness and item 5. Data for Student Equity. Are the examples relevant and realistic, and what

can be gained as a result of "time for reflection" in both items? Clarify your responses.
4. Which of the seven benefits of SEL best enhance student learning and achievement, teacher well-being, and principal leadership? Expound upon your answers.
5. Leading a school is definitely a challenge. The principalship, within the chapter, has been described as a "10,000- aspirin job." Consider the seven identified common challenges a principal faces when initiating and implementing SEL. Based on your experience, which one of the challenges could very well be the greatest principal challenge? Inform and instruct with your response.

CASE STUDY APPLICATION: OVERCOMING THE CHALLENGES, RECOGNIZING THE BENEFITS, AND TEAMING FOR THE SOCIAL AND EMOTIONAL WELL-BEING OF OUR LEARNING COMMUNITY

Principal Catherine Garver, better known as Cissy to her faculty and staff at Giles French School, quickly hurried toward the school's administrative offices. Rain was pouring down as she returned to campus following a lengthy meeting at district offices. Windswept, wet, and attempting to fold her umbrella as she quickly stepped into the campus front office, Dr. Garver was met, first, by her front office receptionist, Anissa Davis. Anissa, seated at her desk, raised her head, greeted her principal with a frown, and then said, with a rolling of eyes, "He's in your office, waiting." The principal looked at her receptionist and nodded her head in affirmation.

Joey Whitaker, mathematics teacher, immediately stood as Dr. Garver entered her office. Joey, a large and somewhat overpowering man, seemed to growl every time he spoke. Today was no exception. "Hello, Dr. Garver. Seems you forgot about our appointment. Afraid to meet with me?" The principal simply shared a cordial hello and took a seat behind her desk. "No, Mr. Whitaker, I didn't forget our appointment, and no, I'm anything but afraid of you," replied the principal. Then, Dr. Garver said, "What can I do for you today, Joey? I believe we just met three days ago. Same subject or a different topic today?"

"Same subject, Cissy." With all formality having obviously been disposed of, Joey Whitaker continued to address his principal. "Let me cut right to the chase, Cissy. There is a great deal of apprehension regarding the newly proposed SEL program. Another new instructional approach to an age-old problem in need of a never-will-happen remedy. Am I right, Cissy, am I right?"

Dr. Garver then stated, "No, Joey, you are not right. As I have shared with you and with all the faculty here at Giles French School, the research is abundantly clear and very straightforward: SEL works, and as an instructional approach, it is a most effective cure when it comes to the well-being of our students and our faculty, too."

Dr. Garver and other members of her administrative team, to include Assistant Principal Bill Keith and academic coach Zulma Diaz, had worked with the faculty for several months in preparation to pilot the new program come next fall semester. It had been an arduous task, demanding long hours of behind-the-scenes efforts before a programmatic roll-out was even considered. Additionally, several weeks working collaboratively with the site-base decision-making team had produced significant buy-in relative to the introduction of SEL as an instructional approach to meeting the varied needs of a diverse student population.

Furthermore, four parent meetings had been held over the last 12 weeks in an effort to communicate programmatic plans and to reach a level of acceptance and support. Finally, departmental meetings with teachers were held weekly throughout the second semester of school; several professional development sessions had been initiated; student forums had been held; and parental, teacher, and student surveys had been administered and tabulated with results disseminated to all parties. Much had been given, all in an effort to make gains in student, teacher, and parental support relative to incorporating the SEL process.

Were there benefits to programmatic inclusion? Absolutely. Were there challenges along the way? Always. Had resistance occurred? Truly. Had acceptance of positive change taken place? In most cases. Still a few resisted. Principal Garver returned her gaze to Joey Whitaker, silently thinking, "Still resisting, are you, Joey?" Then, the principal said to the teacher, "So, Joey, tell me your concern. I'm certain we can find a reasonable and appropriate solution."

APPLICATION QUESTIONS

1. Consider the benefits of Principal Action #4: Appreciate Social and Emotional Learning. Which benefit(s) might Dr. Catherine Garver, principal at Giles French School, best incorporate when working with teacher Joey Whitaker in finding a reasonable and appropriate solution to his resistance? Be specific in your explanation.
2. Reflect upon the school at which you currently serve. How could SEL better advance student learning and achievement, curriculum and instructional advancement, and principal leadership? Be specific in identifying which benefit(s) apply. Explain why.

3. Examine the seven potential distractors/challenges principals must expect and work to avoid when implementing SEL. Which of the seven identified must Dr. Catherine Garver, principal at Giles French School, know, understand, and initiate relative to working with the mathematics teacher, Joey Whitaker? Justify your selection(s).
4. Peruse the chapter section "What Principals Must Know and Understand," specifically examining item 7. Principals Must Lead. Based upon the information provided in the case study, which of the bulleted listings best relate to Principal Garver? Expound upon your answer(s).
5. Contemplate the following: 1) culture and climate improves; 2) mental health is enhanced; 3) student motivation increases; 4) empathy evolves; 5) study habits improve; 6) self-regulation is enhanced; 7) students establish and excel in goal development; and 8) perseverance, resilience, and tenacity are highlighted. Based on your experience, which of the Principal Action #4: Appreciate Social and Emotional Learning benefits outlined above work most effectively in advancing the well-being of students? Teachers?

Chapter 5

Principal Action #5

Distinguish Between Equity and Equality

COMPREHEND THE MEANINGS, UNDERSTAND THE DIFFERENCES, INCORPORATE THE ELEMENTS

"Much has been spoken. Much has been written. Much has transpired. Little has been gained."—Anonymous principal of a southwest middle school

EQUITY IS NOT EQUALITY AND EQUALITY IS NOT EQUITY!

Elizabeth Barrett Browning (1806–1861), English poet whose written works frequently embodied the political and social themes of the day, penned these famous lines: "How do I love thee? Let me count the ways" (PoemHunter.com, 2022). Considering the current political climate and social themes, if not injustices, someone might be compelled to pen, "How am I to accept you? Help me count the ways."

The Latinx principal of a southwest middle school, as noted in the introductory quote, was right. Both time and evidence support his quote, if not his telling case, as much has been written and much has been spoken about the social and political ills of our society. It seems the "much" as described in the previous sentence has only led the staunchest critics of social change and those of the narrowest of minds to contemplate the principal's concluding statement and declare, "Actually, little needs to be gained."

Social justice. Emotional well-being. Individual and collective wellness. Equity, equality, and empathy. Each of these terms, in the hearts and minds of far too many individuals, sadly ring hollow. Why? And just as critical in importance as to the "why" is "how" must the wrongs of today and yesterday be remedied, if not perfected? Either out of absolute ignorance, total crassness, or feigning unawareness, someone might dare to ask, "What wrongs?" A listing of social injustices, albeit incomplete, within and across the United States might prove helpful in responding to the "what wrongs" query:

- Gender inequity
- Ethnicity bias
- Race disparity
- Sexual orientation discrimination
- Religious intolerance
- Nationality resentment
- Ageism
- Poverty tolerance
- Unjust prejudices/policies
- Marginalization of students by policies and practices
- Housing discriminatory practices
- Equality without due recognition of human dignity and respect
- Unequal government regulations
- Mental or physical disabilities
- Insufficient healthcare reform
- Equal pay for equal work
- Voter disenfranchisement
- Other biases, prejudices, and intolerances
- And the list goes on. . . .

PRINCIPAL LEADERSHIP: A MANDATE FOR A BETTER TODAY AND TOMORROW

Reflect back to 1962 and the state of Alabama, where, at the time, only 2 percent of the Black population had the right to vote (U.S. Commission on Civil Rights, n.d.). That's correct—only 2 percent, less than 50 years ago. Today, the dream of having the right to vote for 100 percent of the Black population of Alabama is more than a dream or an idealistic afterthought.

While it is far from an absolute reality, the 100 percent factor, considering the current political climate and voter disenfranchisement efforts, the resolve to change for the better remains a strong conviction and a determination. Sadly, the political deny, delay, and obstruct tactics associated with inequalities and inequities—if not out-and-out racism—will continue, but so shall the will to overcome! It is essential that Principal Action #5: Distinguish Between Equity and Equality be a critical, if not crucial, part of every principal's leadership toolkit.

The history of impoverished races in this country, of children of color and of those who are economically and socially disadvantaged, of those being denied an equal and equitable education could and does fill volumes. Time and history have revealed and many have testified that the journey has been long, arduous, and often traumatic. Serious principal leadership—when it comes to working to overcome institutional and societal inequalities, inequities, and injustices—must be a required and personal mandate.

Granted a trail has been blazed, a path has been beaten, a boardwalk has been built, and a wide concrete walkway has been constructed. This walkway supports many, but it is in need of essential upgrades and repair. The walkway requires additional strengthening, and further expansion and extension, bridging that of yesterday with what today must be more than imagined. Can it occur? Will it happen? Far too often, the answer to those questions is difficult. Yet, those queries, along with so many more, must be addressed.

Come now. Join the journey. Become more than a participant. Lead as a principal advocate and activist. Consider how school leaders can and must take a stand and make a difference when it comes to distinguishing between equity and equality as well as comprehending their meanings, understanding their differences, and incorporating each as an element of much needed change!

Contemplate the messages which rise from the pages of this chapter to further clarify and enlighten principal leadership in today's schools. Recognize there are answers which equate to more than a dream. Can a principal better learn and lead as a result of this chapter reading? Absolutely, as it is a must for the benefit, achievement, advancement, and well-being of all students served!

Return, now, to the introductory quote. Could the principal be correct in his assessment that "little has been gained." Possibly so. However, the ever optimistic might respond, "We may think little has been gained, but we must recognize much more can and will be attained!"

COMPREHEND THE MEANINGS: THE DIFFERENCES BETWEEN EQUITY AND EQUALITY

Equity involves trying to understand and provide individuals, specifically students, with what they need in order to enjoy a full, vibrant, affordable, and rigorous education. Equity is individual-focused, treating each student justly in accordance with their particular circumstance. Equality, in contrast, is group-focused, aiming to ensure that all students achieve the same aspects of fairness in programs, instruction, and well-being in order to enjoy the fullest of opportunities and the most productive of lives.

Equity and Inequity

For purposes of initial examination, consider the term *equity* and its meaning. Equity is defined as a principle of obtaining what is fair—what must be present for there to be equality. While equity is frequently used interchangeably with the related principle of equality, the two terms are not the same. Equity encompasses a wide variety of educational models, programs, and strategies that may be considered fair, but not necessarily equal. It has been noted that equity is the process of obtaining an education; equality is the outcome of said education (Darling-Hammond, 2018).

Inequity occurs when biased or unfair policies, programs, practices, or situations contribute to a lack of equality in student performance, results, and educational outcomes. For example, certain students or groups of students may attend a school, graduate, and ultimately enroll in postsecondary education at lower rates, or they may perform comparatively poorly relative to accountability testing and overall achievement due to a wide variety of factors, including but not limited to inherent biases or flaws, for example, in test designs (Brown Department of Education, 2021; Glossary of Education Reform, 2016).

Equality and Inequality

Equality, on the other hand, is defined as being uniform, level, or evenly balanced. Some might assert that equality is akin to being evenly matched on the playing field or beginning a 40-yard dash at the same starting point—especially in terms of status, rights, and opportunities. For example, the aim, goal, or objective of a principal and members of a learning community is to promote educational similarity or uniformity. Forms of equality, especially in schools, come in terms of social, racial, civil, political, economic, legal, opportunity, and certainly as noted educational and academic.

Inequalities occur when students do not possess the same level of material wealth or overall socioeconomic conditions as related to standards of living, and when there are other disparities in education, health, and/or nutrition. An example of inequality would simply be data which reveals too many student programs in low-income schools are underfunded, illustrating an imbalance between adequate funding for high-income schools and inadequate funding for low-income schools. Therefore, the realization becomes more than apparent: Such is an unfair, thus, unequal practice.

Four Comparative Examples

Recognize the use of Principal Action #5: Distinguish Between Equity and Equality in the following four comparative examples. Equality means each student is provided the same resources and learning opportunities to advance and achieve. Equity recognizes that each student has different circumstances to overcome and thus the allocation of resources and learning opportunities will inevitably be varied. Therefore, said resources and learning opportunities need to be carefully considered and readjusted to promote a parallel and thus corresponding educational outcome.

1. Title 1 funding, which serves to bridge the student achievement gap between what is considered equal educational opportunities and what are, in actuality, unequitable.
2. A school district meeting is held for parents residing in an attendance zone where English is not the primary language for more than 85% of the residents. The meeting is open to all parents, as was the case at other attendance zone meetings across the district. Equal, not equitable. To overcome the inequality issue and make the meeting equitable, the school district leaders hire a translator to attend the meeting and communicate, in the residents' native language, all information that is being imparted.
3. A school district cuts the transportation budget, thus eliminating seven bus routes for a segment of the overall district student population, yet specifically, five of the seven buses serve three low-socioeconomic schools. Equal? Maybe. Equitable? No. To overcome the inequality and ensure equitability, the district determines how certain administrative funds can be reappropriated and thus ensure student transportation to and from all affected schools.
4. A school district has computer labs at all campuses with the same number of computers and the same hours of operation during school hours. Equal? Yes. Equitable? No! To ensure equity, computer labs in lower income attendance zones are provided with more computers as well as longer hours of operation, along with additional laptop computers, as numerous students in these schools do not have access to at-home computers or the Internet.

Bottom line and one final example: There is a difference between equality and equity. Should per-pupil funding at every school be exactly the same?

That is a question of equality. However, should students who attend low socioeconomic, Title 1, and bilingual schools receive additional funding in order to advance and achieve? That is a question of equity.

Why Equity and Equality Matter

First, an important question: Do schools, today, have equity and equality issues? Short answer: Yes! Consider the following as proof. For more than half a century now, the federal government has served to protect "the education of disadvantaged students" according to the Elementary and Secondary Education Act of 1965. Additionally, the Every Student Succeeds Act of 2015 further promotes this ideal. While protection was definitely required 50 years ago, much remains the same today as students far too often require as much educational security and safeguarding.

Reasoning: In 1960, 85.7 percent of public school students were White (Gonzales & Wiener, 2017). Today, the majority of students in public schools are individuals of color. Today, more than half of public school students qualify for free or reduced meals as these students are of low-income families (Gonzales & Wiener, 2017). More than 25 percent of school-age children live in poverty, and if statistics could be even more telling, recognize that students of color are more than twice as likely to be poor (Gonzales & Wiener, 2017).

By any measure, public education has failed when it comes to the equity and equality of student treatment, learning, and achievement (Gonzales & Wiener, 2017). Question: Where does the blame lie? Answer: Definitely consider the following. Politicians at all levels of government are fraught with blame. Additionally, school systems and associated district leadership personnel may very well share the burden of blame. Finally, how about principals? Sadly, yes. Today, there are certain principals who can also accept a share of this blame.

Second, a critical question: What's a principal's role and responsibility as associated with Principal Action #5: Distinguish Between Equity and Equality and in remediating equity and equality issues in schools? Answer A: Recognize that Black and Brown principals are critical for real educational equity and equality. However, understand that these principal leaders of color need support in order to succeed and for their students to succeed. Shelton (2021) relates that authentic connections between principals and students are essential for the overall success of a learning community. Unfortunately, such is not always the case and identified below are the reasons why.

Only 8% of principals across the United States are African American while 15% of students are Black. Only 9% of principals are Hispanic while 30 percent of public school students are Hispanic. These are not only harrowing mismatches, they also represent self-reinforcing insufficiencies that leave students of color farther and farther behind. How, by what means is an attentive query (Shelton, 2021)?

Research has long revealed the profoundly positive impact that Black and Brown principals have on students of color and their achievement. The research has also demonstrated the positive effect principals of color can have on a learning community of color. Black and Brown principals are more effective recruiters of Black and Brown teachers, and they can thus readily establish more trusting relationships with members of a learning community of color. What are school district superintendents and board members to do?

Shelton (2021) reveals that school districts must first increase the number of school leaders of color. Additionally, districts must also ensure that Black- and Brown-led schools succeed and thrive and expand to serve more students of color. An absolute: Principals of color are critical levers in educational equity, equality, and social justice. Therefore, districts must provide required support to these leaders in order that they, their teachers, and their students and community members thrive. Finally, school districts must overcome historical barriers and establish a strong network of support designed to enable principals of color and teachers to do their best work in the service of their students and communities (Shelton, 2021).

Now, returning to the critical question: What's a principal's role and responsibility in remedying equity and equality issues in schools? Answer B: Principals must recognize that every student is different and possesses differing needs. Such a recognition must prompt support and resources. Principals must cultivate a learning community whereby every student feels not only welcomed but listened to and given a voice. Principals must listen, hear, learn from, and respond to students when unfairness abounds. Principals engaging parents of all students—especially those of poverty, low-income, and different languages, cultures, and custom—is an absolute for equity to have a chance to prevail.

Additionally, provide equity and equality training to teachers and staff. Show teachers existing barriers to equality and equity. Barriers include but are not limited to family and society crises, mental health considerations, inadequate healthcare, hunger, homelessness, and English as a second language.

Principals must work collaboratively with teachers and even model diversity and inclusion activities designed to address prejudice, bias, racism, and acts of cruelty against humans in order that students, parents, and all members of the learning community develop a real sense of belonging.

Finally, every principal, and every American for that matter, must come to a reckoning and reach a calculated understanding, an insightful discernment and responsive, if not receptive, belief which openly acknowledges and espouses a mantra explicitly and frequently declared by the late international music star and famed songwriter and legend, Johnny Cash, "God says we are all equal in His eyes and I demand equality" (Cash, 1997)!

Third, an essential question: Why does Principal Action #5: Distinguish Between Equity and Equality matter? Simple answer: Because every student matters! Principals and teams must invest in actions and strategies that are supported by empirical research relative to increased educational opportunities for each student and excellence in academic achievement, as well as societal advancement for all students. Principals and teams must support and develop methods to monitor educational progress and advance schooling improvements toward equity and equality, always holding the entire organization accountable for the well-being of all students.

Specifically, this means rigorous learning opportunities, extensive and effective training of teachers, high-quality instructional resources and funding, student needs support within and outside the school, and system structures that identify areas for positive advancement relative to ensuring students are progressing from elementary to middle to high school and into college, career, and responsible civic engagement.

Returning to the initial query: Why do equity and equality matter? Three significant and requisite responses:

Answer #1: Too many students, especially students of color, are unable to focus on learning due to insufficient technology access, family income limitations, food insecurity, school and community safety concerns, limited if not unequal and inequitable assessment measures, inadequate instructional funding and resources, insufficient rigor to support immediate learning needs, unreinforced norms for appropriate student actions and behaviors, and a narrowing of student monitoring practices. Each of these factors provides compelling examples as to why equity and equality matter yet inequity and inequality permeate the American education system, our society, and our political system.

Answer #2: Time pressures, deficient teacher training and professional development, continuous changing of school leaders (frequently associated with transfers, resignations, promotions, and/or burnout), non-stimulating teaching strategies, inadequate curriculum revisionary practices, insufficient peer feedback, reduced student discourse opportunities, eroded pedagogy, and limitations in how teachers engage and interact with students in both online and face-to-face learning environments reveal why equity and equality matter. Each of these points serves to further create inequities and inequalities in leading, learning, and instruction.

Answer #3: The continued dissemination of packets of worksheets for independent seatwork; reduced teacher creativity and resourcefulness due to stringent accountability goals, objectives, and standards; diminished site-based decision-making with ever-advancing top-down dictates and encroachment practices; along with a myriad of other hurdles continue to mitigate equality concerns and further advance inequities for all students across the United States.

To quote Malcolm X, "We can't teach what we don't know, and we can't lead where we can't go" (AZ Quotes, 2021b). Jesse Jackson incorporated a variation of this quote: "You can't teach what you don't know. And you can't lead where you don't go" (AZ Quotes, 2021a). Equity and equality matter—it's a simple statement of fact. Again, what's a principal to do?

For additional information and detail regarding equity, and more specifically racial equity, see the FutureEd study *Changing the Narrative: The Push for New Equity Measures in Education* (2021) by Lynn Olson and Thomas Toch, a read well worth the time with corresponding National Academies Proposed Indicators of Educational Equity (see pages 14–15).

SUPPORT SOCIAL JUSTICE: THE EQUITY-EQUALITY-EMPATHY RELATIONSHIP

Principals must recognize there exist alternate methods of learning and leading as related to Principal Action #5: Distinguish Between Equity and Equality. David DeMatthews in his book *Community Engaged Leadership for Social Justice* (2018) writes:

> Racial achievement and discipline gaps persist. Students of color are disproportionately identified into special education and educated in separate classrooms and schools. Culturally and linguistically diverse students are frequently viewed as testing liabilities in need of intervention, rather than students with unique and valuable assets. A hidden curriculum pervades classrooms and socializes low-income students of color in ways that maintain rather than transform the status quo. (p. ix)

Moreover, principals readily relate the importance of parents relative to school improvement and student academic achievement, yet in practice, far too many Black, Latinx, and low-income parents are viewed as deficient (DeMatthews, 2019). Where is equity, equality, and/or empathy as opposed to the regular lip service imparted by far too numerous school leaders? To coin a term from the Latin, *in absentia*!

What Is Social Justice?

Social justice is the view that everyone deserves equal economic, political, and social rights and opportunities. Social justice imposes on every individual a personal responsibility to work with others to design school programs, to continually perfect instruction, and to teach all students for not only personal development but for social enhancement and advancement.

While formal definitions of social justice vary, there are commonalities worthy of identification. Such commonalities or principles, especially as related to schooling, include:

1. equal rights
2. equitable opportunities
3. equal treatment

Five additional commonalities or principles associated with social justice in education are access to funding and resources, equity, participation, diversity, and student rights.

Simply put, social justice in education, from an administrative perspective, refers to a commitment from principals to actively challenge social, cultural, and economic inequalities that have been imposed on students based on any differential distribution of power, resources, or privilege. More specifically, from a contradictory standpoint, social injustice in schools has to be combatted by principals relative to neighborhoods of inopportunity, racial segregation, school reform and reorganization inactions, and school failures as social institutions of positive change.

Principal leadership, from a social justice outlook, must take responsibility for bringing justice to injustice by 1) not isolating those already isolated, denied, deprived, and dehumanized; 2) understanding backgrounds and conditions detrimental to progress; 3) working to bring light onto the rights of so many wronged—to transform, to bring to a better place, to rectify the past treatment of the persecuted, the victimized, and the wounded; 4) bearing responsibility for personal sins of recognized and even-unrecognized wrongdoings and behaviors, as well as the sins of our fathers; and 5) changing for the better through individual as well as collective actions (DeMatthews, 2019). Yes, it is a tough pill to swallow, but one that must be taken!

Equity, Equality, and Empathy: Essential in Overcoming Bias, Prejudice, and Discrimination

To overcome personal or organizational bias, prejudice, and/or discrimination, it is critical to identify, acknowledge, and eliminate each. What are the types of bias, prejudice, and discrimination?

Types of Bias, Prejudice, and Discrimination

Bias types include:

- overconfidence
- self-serving
- herd mentality
- loss aversion
- narrative fallacy
- anchoring
- confirmation
- hindsight
- optimism/pessimism
- tribalism

Prejudice types include:

- racism
- sexism
- ageism
- classism
- homophobia
- nationalism
- xenophobia
- linguistic

Discrimination types are:

- disability
- sexual orientation
- religion
- national origin
- pregnancy
- sexual harassment

Overcoming bias, prejudice, and/or discrimination, past or present, requires principals to incorporate the 3Es: equity, equality, and empathy. To do so, follow the TOP-10 Steps to Quality Leadership as prescribed by Landau (2021), Cherry (2020), and Mungal and Sorenson (2020). School leaders must initiate Principal Action #5: Distinguish Between Equity and Equality by:

1. gaining support and awareness for anti-prejudice social norms from stakeholders within and across the learning community
2. increasing interactions with other social groups and cultures outside the school building

3. helping stakeholders recognize inconsistencies relative to their own values and beliefs
4. aiding in district policy development and campus regulations which require fair and equal treatment for all groups and cultures
5. recognizing their own personal conscious and unconscious biases and seeking help and training to overcome said biases
6. working to increase empathy and empathic communication with all members of the learning community
7. practicing mindfulness and loving-kindness in all faculty and parent interactions
8. developing cross-culture friendships
9. recognizing that discrimination is unacceptable in all its forms and has no place within or across the school community
10. being proactive and taking action which supports equity and equality

Vulnerable Students

According to the Organisation for Economic Co-operation and Development (OECD) and the National Center for Children in Poverty, the nation's most vulnerable students are those living in chronic poverty (15 million or one in five), homeless (2.5 million), living with untreated mental health issues (17 million with depression, anxiety, or other conditions), in foster care (460,000), Black (7.7 million), Latinx (14 million), Native American (0.5 million), children with diverse gender identities, special education students, refugee children, and immigrant children (17.8 million) (Howard, 2018; National Center for Education Statistics, 2021; OECD, 2021).

Immigrant Students: Challenges Abound

Immigrant students and their families are coming into the United States, legally (77 percent) and illegally and for various reasons, notably, seeking greater economic opportunity and often asylum. Budiman (2020), conducting research for the Pew Research Center, reveals that 45 million immigrants reside in the United States (half of which are from Mexico and other Latin American countries). More than 1 million immigrants arrive in the United States annually.

These students frequently confront overwhelming challenges, including interrupted schooling, learning a second language, and experiencing medical needs and psychological trauma. They often have to attend immigration court hearings and, sadly, far too many decide they need an income-earning job rather than a high school diploma. Most of the students are coming from Mexico and the Northern Triangle (El Salvador, Guatemala, and Honduras).

In 2021, almost 400,000 immigrant students were enrolled in public schools in the United States. California and Texas each enroll about 50,000 of these students, the bulk in schools in Los Angeles and Houston (Kaufman & Culbertson, 2021).

Yes, challenges abound—for both immigrant students and schools. Schools, for example, require more teachers, counselors, and principals to meet an immigration trend that is far from abating. However, schools are not funded to staff and support the growing immigrant population. Funding policies must change and change quickly if schools, as well as politicians and governmental entities, expect academic success and achievement for all students.

One final challenge: Teachers feel inadequate and underequipped to address academic, language, and the social and emotional needs of immigrant students. Many teachers of immigrant students do not speak the home language of these newly arrived learners. Teachers also need training in trauma-informed instruction to adapt to the learning needs of distressed immigrant students.

Immigration Is More Than a Border Issue: Inequities, Inequalities, and Exclusions

RAND Corporation researchers revealed that an estimated 321,000 undocumented and asylum-seeking students enrolled in U. S. public schools between 2016 and 2019 (Napolitano, 2021). The vast majority of immigrant students reside with families (in descending order) in Florida, California, Texas, and New York, followed by Georgia, North Carolina, and Virginia.

According to Las Americas Immigrant Advocacy Center (2021), based in El Paso, Texas, public education offers immigrant families and their children a gateway to advancement in life and career, along with valued social capital and intergenerational mobility. Yet, immigrant students face far too many challenges to successfully integrate into and engage in schooling, let alone earn a high school diploma or college degree.

Additionally, immigrant students have higher drop-out rates, especially compared to their native-born peers. The hurdles for immigrant students are incalculable. The language barrier is immense. Academic success is often fleeting. Institutional and social inclusion is repeatedly futile. Inequities, inequalities, and exclusions are regularly recurrent (KIND, 2021). What's a principal to do?

Help Those Who Think It's Hopeless

As previously noted, more than 17 million immigrant students are in public schools today. These students are by far our nation's most vulnerable, and whatever political persuasion and personal values and beliefs are possessed regarding immigrants to this country, immigrant students are in great need of principal-led equity, equality, empathy, and inclusion.

To meet the educational, social, emotional, behavioral, and health needs of immigrant students, principals and instructional teams must actively engage in policy and regulation options, always serving as an advocate of support for immigrant students. OECD (2021) has identified a listing of school-oriented criteria selections principals must adapt to, if not actually adopt, when working with not only immigrant students, but with all vulnerable students.

- Implement instructional initiatives which are dedicated to improving social and emotional needs.
- Include all relevant stakeholders for inclusion in policy design, curriculum renewal, and instructional implementation.
- Develop anti-bullying campaigns and anti-discriminatory policies.
- Facilitate communication and strong partnerships between schools and families and communities.
- Develop relationships between appropriate child-oriented agencies and school.
- Encourage schooling by introducing a system of limited absenteeism incentives.
- Address learning gaps with "catch-up" instructional strategies.
- Support non-formal learning activities such as after-school tutoring, peer tutoring, coaching, summer camps, and special learner-focused clubs.
- Support extracurricular activities to better increase student interest in schooling.
- Prioritize the teaching of civic education, acknowledging and embracing all peoples in society, regardless of legal citizenship status (Banks & Banks, 2021).
- Improve the access to and quality of distance learning.
- Offer to the most vulnerable students hybrid model teaching and learning methods and strategies.
- Mandate extensive monitoring and evaluation initiatives to best ensure academic gaps of the vulnerable students are identified and extensively addressed.
- Show and demand—through instructional programs and teaching—equity, equality, and empathy.

Reflect upon these words from a 17-year-old immigrant student, Sua Ramos: "I ask them to be patient with us. It's not like we are dumb or something. It's just there's a language barrier. Give us a chance. Don't think of us as aliens. We are people who want a better life" (Napolitano, 2021, p. 4).

HOW TO ROOT OUT RACISM IN SCHOOLS

The European Commission against Racism and Intolerance ([ECRI] 2021), Howard (2018), Jones (2020), and Superville (2020) all reiterate a long-known fact: Racism, sadly and far too often tragically, remains a serious impediment to American life and to all peoples, specifically people of color. Today, people of color observe, with regularity, the continuous acts of demagoguery; the ugly, racist dogwhistles in political speech; as well as the flagrant disregard for and disrespect of others who are perceived as "different" in color, language, clothing, socioeconomic status, and culture.

Institutional racial ills, as related to education, continue today. For example, institutional racial barriers can be found in school systems throughout the country when examining disproportionate and inadequate school funding formulas, and in ongoing debates about what students should be taught regarding slavery and racism.

Moreover, in 2021 alone, legislative bills limiting how educators can teach about racism were introduced in 28 states (Ramirez, 2021) including bills restricting how not only race, but history is taught. All of this often leads to misinterpretation and much confusion, and ultimately, negative consequences for teachers and principals (Chavez, 2021; Killough, 2021).

People of color are understandably drained; they are tired of continually attempting to describe, plead, and articulate the realities, the inequities, and inequalities of racism. Yet, the fight for social justice continues as prejudice, bigotry, intolerance, biases, and discriminatory practices remain. Even principals of color, particularly Black school leaders, are under tremendous pressure due to racial tensions over diversity hiring to better reflect student demographics (DeMatthews & Clarida, 2021).

Howard (2018) asserts a truism: Racism will never end until all peoples, especially Whites, feel just as upset about the realities and effects of racism as people of color feel. The critical question: What's a principal to do? Posed another way, how should a principal lead in response when attempting to ensure Principal Action #5: Distinguish Between Equity and Equality and overcome racism? Superville (2020) and Jones (2020) provide expert guidance in responding to the previous two queries.

First, principals must address racism in their schools with faculty, students, parents, and community members. Principals must lead teachers in doing the same in every classroom. To do less is to fail as a school leader. Principals can pave the way to eradicating racism by working and interacting with the current generation of students and by allowing students to talk about their feelings, to write about their emotions, and to be provided space to simply emote.

Second, principals must recognize students of color are not only bitter in thoughts and feelings, but they are also emotionally fragile. The bluster, the demonstrations, the speeches, the outrage is real but often a cover for the tenuous, precarious, and breakable feelings of the inner-self. There is fear, anger, anxiety, sadness, grief, and conviction. Students of color need principals to listen, to hear their pleas for change. Students of color need to be affirmed in these precarious times. The one thing students of color do not wish or want from their school leader, or their classroom teacher is a return to business as usual.

Third, principals must challenge the notion, the long-embedded thinking, that this too shall pass. Racism has not passed. It is as present today as it was yesterday and the yesterdays before. Racism is persistent, ever lingering. Racism is ugly, often deadly. Racism develops a vociferous and tangled web of deceit that targets, dehumanizes, and frequently murders fellow Americans (Advancement Project, 2021; National Association for the Advancement of Colored People, 2021).

Fourth, principals must take charge and lead with conviction if racism is to be eradicated from schooling and if racism is to be eradicated from the minds of the generation of students served. This country has overcome the terrible affects of polio and other childhood diseases, is working to rid the deadly COVID-19 virus and variants on a daily basis. There is no reason that racism cannot and should not be eradicated—killed out and forever forbidden in the life of every person residing in this country. Transformative and collective action is required! Again, the question persists: What's a principal to do? How? By what means?

Fifth, here's a start; a principal's to-do list:

- Create, enforce, and fund policies, procedures, and campus regulations associated with equality, equity, and empathy, and, thus, eliminate discrimination.
- Train teachers and staff members to work with and accept students from all nationalities, ethnic groups, races, creeds, genders, and other backgrounds.
- Include parents and community members of color and other cultures in site-based decision-making as it relates to promoting equality, equity, empathy, and non-discriminatory campus practices and procedures.
- Work with school district administration to develop mandates which oppose racism and discrimination of any form—especially as related to accepting and tolerating student diversity.
- Ensure, monitor, and verify that appropriate teaching methods, strategies, techniques, and practices are incorporated into the campus curriculum

and instructional program—all of which began at the pre-kindergarten level and are reflective of the diversity and plurality of society.
- Adopt and enforce an anti-racist and anti-discrimination code of conduct for not only students but for school personnel as well.
- Monitor and eliminate all racist incidents within the school.
- Develop data analyses/dashboards (attendance, drop-out rates, and academic performance, for example) which allow for the careful monitoring of key statistics relative to minority students.
- Avoid any segregation of students with special needs as well as minority students into separate classrooms or classroom instructional groups/subsets.
- Actively incorporate bilingual education programs which promote English language acquisition for minority and immigrant students.
- Recruit teachers from minority groups as well as differing cultures.
- Actively and regularly promote equality, equity, and empathy awareness programs.
- Ensure and verify that teachers are trained in and implementing preventive programs as related to any potential manifestations of racism and racial discrimination.
- React promptly, appropriately, and expertly when faced with any manifestations of campus racism and racial discrimination (ECRI, 2021; Jones, 2020).

Sixth, recognize that there is a great need for education and awareness programs in schools to prevent racism, racial discrimination, and hate crimes. Sadly, even today—especially in light of extremist political propaganda and anti-immigrant rhetoric—principals must be diligent in their efforts to contain and eliminate any and all disruptive systems of inequity and inequality.

Finally, recall three truisms, quotes that are most appropriate today: "Our ability to reach unity in diversity will be the beauty and the test of our civilization" (Mahatma Gandhi, 1925; Notable Quotes [2022]), "It is never too late to give up your prejudices" (Henry David Thoreau; BrainyQuote, [2021a]), and "To know what is right and not to do it is the worst cowardice" (Confucius; QuotePark.com [2021]).

CONCLUDING COMMENTS

Individuals of substance can often be identified as good people with great intentions who gain meaningful and long-lasting results. Deep-rooted institutional structures have perpetuated society, life, and even organizations with racial bias and discriminatory practices. Yet, if school principals—working collaboratively with faculty, students, parents, and community members—are willing to seek an opportunity to step into the dangers and difficulties of racist turmoil and do what is right, just, moral, and ethical, a greater good can and will prevail.

FINAL THOUGHTS

Exceptional principals recognize the difference between equity and equality and, furthermore, understand that far too many social injustices plague the nation and school systems as well. All too frequently, certain aspects of society resonate a denial of reality when it comes to equity, equality, and racism and, moreover, delay admitting reality, and sadly, obstruct accepting reality.

Exceptional school leaders initiate Principal Action #5: Distinguish Between Equity and Equality. They are aware of and work to overcome the long history of impoverished races in this country, of children of color and those who are economically and socially disadvantaged being denied an equal and equitable education. These school leaders comprehend and address the differences between equity and inequity, equality and inequality, and initiate training, programs, and teaching methods, strategies, and techniques which address why equity and equality matter in public schooling.

Exceptional principals support social justice—in the forms of equal rights, equitable opportunities for all, and equal treatment—to overcome bias, prejudice, and discrimination. These principals readily identify and combat types of bias, prejudice, and discrimination, following a TOP-10 Steps to Quality Leadership which serves to gain support and awareness for anti-racist social norms and behaviors.

Exceptional principals adopt a 14-point school-oriented process to eradicate racism in schools and schooling. They also commit to six critical standards: 1) address racism, 2) recognize the emotional fragility resulting from racism, 3) challenge long-embedded institutional barriers, 4) take charge and lead with conviction to overcome racism in schools, 5) utilize a 14-point to-do list for overcoming racism in schooling, and 6) recognize there is a great need for education and awareness programs in schools to prevent racism, racial discrimination, extremist political propaganda, anti-immigrant rhetoric, and hate crimes.

DISCUSSION QUESTIONS

1. Contemplate Principal Action #5: Distinguish Between Equity and Equality. Explain how equity and equality are different. Identify which

of the 18 social injustices listed earlier in the chapter are prevalent in your community, in your school. Explore, in writing, how a principal can address said injustices at the school and community levels.
2. Debate the proposition that school principals must be public advocates and activists regarding injustices and equity and equality issues in school and society.
3. Why do equity and equality matter in society, in schools? Explain.
4. What is social justice and how does it correlate with equity, equality, and empathy? Clarify.
5. Examine the chapter section regarding the types of bias, prejudice, and discrimination. Which of each category are most prevalent today, both throughout society and in education? Provide evidence for your reasoning.
6. Which of the TOP-10 Steps to Quality Leadership do you perceive to be absolutes to effective and essential principal leadership? Expound and enlighten.
7. Consider the most vulnerable students in your school today. The OECD has identified a listing of school-oriented criteria that principals must adopt. Which 5 of the 14 identified are most critical to principal leadership in helping the hopeless?
8. Reflect upon the principal's to-do list in the chapter section entitled "How to Root Out Racism in Schools." Of the 14 listed, which ones should the principal at your school incorporate? Explain why.

CASE STUDY APPLICATION: RETHINKING BOUNDARIES, BUILDING A FRAMEWORK FOR RACIAL EQUITY, EQUALITY, AND EMPATHY

"We are rethinking boundaries," said Pete Dixon, teacher at Walt Whitman School and member of the equity-focused decision-making team. Liz McIntyre, school principal, simply smiled and replied, "Yes, significant progress is being made. This is a great team and I'm proud of the work we are accomplishing." The team consisted of Pete Dixon, teacher; Helen Loomis, counselor; Alice Johnson, teacher; Josh Allen, student; and Liz McIntyre, principal.

Each of the team members had been working every day after school for several weeks, always meeting in Room 222, a multi-purpose room often used on campus for professional development sessions. About that time, school superintendent Seymour Kaufman stepped in and showcased a wide grin, saying, "I thought I'd find all of you in here. I'm anxious to learn what progress has been made. You all know the floodlights are on our educational system and more so on Walt Whitman School. Tell me, what has transpired since I was here last week? You all were working on a common thread at the time."

Pete Dixon replied, "Deep, difficult reflection which has resulted in a common-threaded six-point process to build racial equity. We're the model school and we are just about ready to pilot this program for the entire school district." The work had been arduous and at times more than difficult—sometimes contentious. But the results have been well conceived and methodically developed.

The team at Walt Whitman School believed they had written, developed, and committed to a plan that would effectively promote equity in not only Walt Whitman School but in every school across the district. "Tell me about the progress made, the plan you all have designed and developed, and how it will help us promote equity, equality, and empathy," said Superintendent Kaufman.

Principal McIntyre began the discussion but soon encouraged each of the team members to communicate the accomplished work. The initiated, yet lengthy and robust discussion soon culminated with team members identifying the following six-point process to building racial equity (see Notes):

1. *Define the terms*: equity, equality, empathy, tolerance, racially diverse educational setting, race relations, diversity, the rights of others, and a continuing list of related terms. Principals, working collaboratively with members of a school, must ensure that the terminology related to the well-being of a learning community is appropriately defined, relevant in purpose, and applicable in usage and practice relative to teaching, learning, and leading.
2. *Enlist community expertise and support*: Racism is a scourge, a plague—an offensive tormentor cursing humanity. Equity, on the other hand, ensures diversity in thought, relationships, and inclusionary practices. When principals and teams enlist community involvement, an embracing of knowledge, capability, cooperation, and support results.
3. *Confront all boundaries, barriers, resources, and staffing*: Change is all about rethinking the impossible. Over the years, schooling, for the most part, hasn't changed all that much. Barriers block what is good. Change brings advancement. Remember, when in doubt, choose change when contemplating all aspects of schooling, especially as it relates to the equal and equitable well-being of all stakeholders. Progress is the recognition that any one individual must always rethink things that have already been thought through.

4. *Establish a framework for decision-making*: Develop matrices which measure how decisions are made, who is affected, and for what purposes and reasons. Essential, effective decision-making requires this question: "Are diverse voices represented in solutions?" Quick decision-making can be a hindrance, especially as related to equity, equality, empathy, and well-being. There are times when a slow decision-making process provides for appropriate, thoughtful, and respectful problem-solving.
5. *Identify critical questions to be posed and answered*: One very important question and consideration a principal and team must consider is: "Is the decision, the change, the improvement culturally responsive, inclusive, empathetic, equitable, and equal in the eyes of all stakeholders?" If the answer results in even the slightest pause, rethink the decision immediately. Remember, critical questions enlighten, and relevant answers illuminate!
6. *Create an equity analyses system*: Data must be utilized and incorporated for the purpose of inclusion, not exclusion. System-wide, learning community–wide evaluative measures with equity as a guide must serve as a principal's north star. Follow the 8-Point School Leadership Compass: 1) Believe and achieve when all seems unattainable; 2) make determination a guiding strength; 3) recognize that small progress totals big results; 4) understand that magnanimity is a corresponding word to empathy; 5) ensure the hard work benefits all, especially the vulnerable; 6) acknowledge mastery begins with humility so stay humble; 7) realize kindness overcomes hatred, and 8) keep on keeping on because tenacity is a principal's ability to hang on when letting go appears most attractive (Samuels, 2020; Sorenson, 2022).

APPLICATION QUESTIONS

1. Review the six-point process to building racial equity as identified in the case study. Which of the six is absolutely critical to principal leadership when addressing racial inequity, inequality, and racism? Provide an exploratory analysis.
2. Which of the six-point process listings best correlates with principal leadership and Principal Action #5: Distinguish Between Equity and Equality when combating social injustices? Justify your answer.
3. Identify which of the six-point processes reveal parallel linkages with the TOP-10 Steps to Quality Leadership. Explain why.
4. Immigrant students in the United States often feel hopeless for a variety of reasons, as detailed within the chapter. The OECD has identified a listing of school-oriented criteria that principals should adopt when

working with vulnerable students. Which of the OECD criteria relate to the six-point process to building racial equity?
5. Examine the principal's to-do list to eradicating racism in school and the community. Which of the six-point processes connect with the to-do listing? Provide a comparative analysis.
6. Think through and discuss: Identify tenets or principles of empathy, equality, and equity. How do each correlate with inclusivity and accessibility, and how do each relate to the needs of immigrant students as well as other diverse learners?

Chapter 6

Principal Action #6

Ensure Empathy Is a Campus and Cultural Norm

"Empathy. Could a greater miracle take place than for us to look through each other's eyes for an instant?"—Henry David Thoreau (1817–1862) (BrainyQuote, 2021a)

WHAT IS EMPATHY?

Empathy has been defined as the ability to step into the shoes of another person, aiming to understand their feelings and perspectives, and to use that understanding to guide personal actions (World Book Dictionary, 2019). Former President Barack Obama shared, "Learning to stand in somebody else's shoes, to see through their eyes, that's how peace begins. Empathy is a quality of character that can change the world. And it's up to you to make that happen" (Quotefancy.com, 2021).

Henry David Thoreau, an American naturalist, essayist, poet, author, and philosopher, was absolutely correct more than 150 years ago when he revealed that no greater miracle could occur than for mankind to see, just for one moment, what life is like for those who live in fear, hopelessness, neglect, and possible abandonment.

Many have never experienced such feelings of despair. Yet, we should empathize with those who do. We must learn, if we do not know how, to understand, to relate, to identify with, to feel for, and to have compassion for that which we have not seen, lived, or that which we might simply want to wish away or, sadly, choose to ignore. School leaders must incorporate Principal Action #6: Ensure Empathy Is a Campus and Cultural Norm.

Elements of Empathy and Why Empathy Is Not Sympathy

First, empathy is not sympathy and sympathy is not empathy! The difference between the two terms can be summed up in four words: "poor you" and "really difficult." When one sympathizes, the first thought, judgment, is "poor you." When empathizing, there is no judgment call, just an understanding of how "really difficult" it must be for the individual (Kisling, 2021).

Second, empathy involves understanding *why* an individual feels a particular way, recognizing the root cause of the individual's feelings and more significantly, what can be done to better understand the person and circumstances and, thus, how to provide healthier, if not healing options. Four initial attributes of empathy are as follows: 1) take perspective, 2) remain nonjudgmental, 3) recognize an individual's emotional quotient, and 4) communicate a genuine understanding of the individual's emotional state.

Third, seven elements, according to Raman (2012) and Nachin and Sorenson (2021), of empathy, from the perspective of a principal leader, are to:

1. *Display emotional intelligence*: by possessing the traits and social skills to understand non-verbal signals, body language, and facial expressions and then to respond appropriately to another's emotions.
2. *Possess a mindset*: by connecting at the right moment and with the right attitude, to another individual who is in the greatest of need.
3. *Be present:* by being mindful of the here and now. Being attentive to the present moment and aware of an individual's feelings.
4. *Pay attention:* by showing a genuine interest and by being a source of encouragement at the moment of need, and then, carefully listening, prudently hearing, and sincerely understanding.
5. *Respond respectfully:* by being heartfelt and earnest in actions and reactions. Sometimes, respectfully pausing will elicit even more of a response.
6. *Encourage and support:* by providing supportive comments, as required, such as "I see," "Really," or "Please continue." Otherwise, utilize gestures such as nodding affirmatively, maintaining eye contact, and showing through facial expressions a genuine regard for the individual and what is being shared.
7. *Elicit feelings:* by bringing out the feelings of another, utilizing phrases such as "I see that you are angry" or "I'm sorry but something seems to be upsetting you" or "I recognize that you are hurt."

EMPATHY: A CRITICAL TOOL FOR EFFECTIVE SCHOOL LEADERSHIP

Here's a surprising tidbit of information: Ineffective leaders make up half of today's organizations, to include schools (Gentry, Weber, & Sadri, 2016). Underperformance has been credited to a lack of empathy. What is an absolute: Many leadership theorists suggest that the ability to have and demonstrate empathy is an essential leadership skill. What is known is that empathy positively relates to effective leadership performance.

Principals who are empathetic show greater interest in the needs and hopes of others; are willing to assist teachers and students with personal issues; convey compassion; create more loyal, engaged, and productive teams; increase organizational content and happiness; foster innovation through collaboration and communication; know and understand others better; avoid judgmental thinking, listen more, and talk less; and recognize the needs of others.

Types of Empathy

Mediate Your Life (2015) identifies four types of empathy, each of which plays an essential leadership role when it comes to the social and emotional well-being of a school's learning community. Stakeholders need encouragement, understanding, and a welcoming principal who possesses a listening ear. These school leaders frequently exhibit, all depending on the situation, one or more of the following types of empathy:

- *Awareness Empathy*. A principal is aware and attentive to what is being shared. This principal is focused and visually aware of the nonverbal body language of an individual in peril and all the while remains non-judgmental.
- *Silent Empathy*. A principal is very attuned, silently keying in on what is at the heart of the matter or problem. Here, a principal listens and observes, always seeking those true, yet often hidden, feelings, needs, desires, or requests of others.
- *Reflective Empathy*. Reality and meaning are critical components of a principal recognizing what is clearly indicative or true as resonated by a troubled individual. When a principal can understand, can see the tree for the forest, and then reflect by having observed and heard the not so obvious, the leader is able to enrich the well-being of an individual, and, thus, reflective empathy has occurred.

- *Verbal Empathy.* Developing a deeper connection with another individual sometimes requires a principal to verbally insert words of compassion, responsiveness, and identification into conversations. Such statements include but are not limited to the following:
  - I understand how you feel.
  - You're making total sense.
  - You must feel so hopeless.
  - I'm on your side.
  - I'm listening and I hear you.
  - Oh my, that sounds terrible.
  - I totally agree with you.
  - That sounds so frustrating.
  - That would upset me as well.
  - No wonder you're upset.
  - That must have hurt.
  - I admire what you are doing.
  - I would have been disappointed, too.
  - Tell me what you think are your choices.
  - I wish you didn't have to go through that.
  - I understand why you are feeling so trapped.
  - I wish I could have been with you in that moment.
  - I see. Let me summarize what I believe you are sharing with me.

Signs of Empathy

Principals who are empathetic toward students, teachers, and parents readily pay attention. They are reflective in conversations, saying, "What I hear you saying is . . ." These principals clarify what they may not understand by asking faculty and staff to repeat or clarify. In other words, they are not primadonnas or know-it-alls. These school leaders share, especially a recognition of the accomplishments of others, and they are active participants engaged in leading curriculum development and renewal, in leading instructional changes and innovations, in leading professional development, and in leading with empathy and understanding.

These same principals exhibit or signify empathy by taking into account the personal experiences (good and bad) of others, by cultivating compassion, by honing the skills of others, by promoting others and their good works, and by building and maintaining relationships with teachers, students, and parents. Empathetic principals take time from their busy schedule to interact with students, teachers, custodians, maintenance workers, and family members of students and faculty and are genuine in their behaviors and actions.

Common Barriers to Empathetic Leadership

Aparna Joshi Khandwala (2020), human resource expert, writes that an empathetic leader can make personnel feel like a team, increase productivity, better deal with failures, enhance individual performance, better manage employees, contribute more effectively, improve organizational morale, help students better achieve, and make all stakeholders feel welcomed, appreciated, safe, and secure. Yet not all principals are natural-born empathetic persons. That said, what creates barriers to empathy for those leaders who fail to possess this essential skill?

Khandwala (2020) and Sorenson and Goldsmith (2009) identify seven barriers to empathy that regrettably serve to block principals from engaging in effective school leadership. Can these barriers be overcome? The answer is yes. How? Consider the following barriers and then examine the next chapter section, "Can Empathy Be Developed? How to Overcome Being an Unempathetic Principal."

1. *Fear*. I don't fail. You might, but I don't.
2. *Belittling Attitude*. That's not my problem.
3. *Comparative Comments*. You're no _____ (fill in a name).
4. *Poor Listening Habits*. Please, I don't have time to listen to that.
5. *Judgmental*. He's lazy. That's why he can't manage his students.
6. *Finger-Pointing*. Well, if you don't have a solution to your problem, don't expect me to come up with one.
7. *Harsh Choice of Words*. I know she has problems at home. She always does. Hey, don't we all?

Can Empathy Be Developed? How to Overcome Being an Unempathetic Principal

Some principals are simply not born being empathetic. It's not a part of their DNA. That is unfortunate, especially from a leadership perspective, but recognize it is a trait that can be improved upon, if not actually developed. Listed below are a baker's dozen of recommendations to follow when seeking to become an empathetic leader:

1. Seek additional training.
2. Consider therapeutic approaches.
3. Develop broader perspectives.
4. Be learning community focused.
5. Empower others.

6. Be more flexible.
7. Work on being less selfish.
8. Become more approachable.
9. Develop a higher self-esteem.
10. Become a servant leader.
11. Involve others in problem-solving and decision-making.
12. Learn from the examples of mentors and/or other principals.
13. Recognize the need to change from being the professor to becoming the pupil.

SEVEN HABITS OF HIGHLY EMPATHETIC PRINCIPALS

Empathy is the glue that holds the school organization together. Principal empathy makes for positive, productive, and long-term relationships. Empathy allows students, teachers, parents, and community members to feel accepted and validated. Empathy builds trust. Empathy comforts, motivates, and defuses tension. Empathy, as a principal action, cultivates effort, productivity, and ensures organizational achievement. Empathy creates positivity, generates happiness, and instigates success. The very best principals exude habits of empathy. Here are seven habits worthy of consideration, coming from the likes of human resource executives, school personnel professors, psychologists, and executive coaches (Jaitely, 2020; Khandwala, 2020; Richard, 2021; Sorenson & Goldsmith, 2009; Wilding, 2019).

- Habit #1: Focus on the individual. Make that one person feel like she or he is the most important person. Make them feel like they are the best. Provide the individual with the gift of full attention and respect. Both the person and the organization receives a boost!
- Habit #2: Ensure individuals have the freedom to share their feelings openly, knowing they will not be judged or criticized. Permit emotions to flow freely, creating a gateway to productive problem-solving.
- Habit #3: Avoid offering opinions. Ask questions to better understand the perspectives of others.
- Habit #4: Ensure people feel empowered and supported. Leading is a team sport, and remember, with empathy, there is no "I" in "team"!
- Habit #5: Step into another person's shoes and imagine what they are facing. The best intent is providing individuals with the benefit of the doubt and ensuring they sense respect, not maliciousness.
- Habit #6: Be reflective ("It sounds to me like you're saying . . ."). Be affirming (smile, nod, and state, "I see" or "I understand"). And always

be encouraging ("I believe there's a solution to the problem and we can work it out").
- Habit #7: Recall the Golden Rule: *Do unto others as you would have them do unto you.* In other words, treat others the way you want to be treated. Then, remember the Platinum Rule: *Treat others the way they want, and need, to be treated.*

THE SCHOOL CLIMATE CHALLENGE: ENSURING EMPATHY IS A NORM

Today, the principalship is a challenging role, responsibility, and endeavor. Such a position requires school districts to hire and develop more effective instructional leaders who are capable of successfully moving campus organizations and students forward. To do so requires searching for individuals who are adept beyond traditional leadership strategies and who are proficient at cultivating those critical skills most essential for guiding students and faculties to success. Perhaps unexpectedly, one of those skills is empathy—a vital leadership competency. Empathy in the principalship is positively related to successful job performance.

Recall, empathy refers to the ability or skill to experience, to understand, to relate to the emotions, ideas, or opinions of others. Empathetic principals are able to connect with others in such a manner that relationships are enhanced, and performances are further developed and ultimately improved. The result is a more positive climate and open culture. The question begging an answer: How does a principal build a climate and culture of empathy?

Building a Climate and Culture of Empathy

First, principals must be observant of teacher burnout—a real problem in schools today! Teacher pressures and stresses—often associated with mandated testing and accountability, overexceeding parental influence, student disciplinary issues, difficulties on the home front, increased workloads, and overwork—frequently handicap principals and, yes, students, with an increase in faculty turnover rates.

Now, add into the equation those principals who are overbearing, uncaring, selfish, and egotistical. Well, that's akin to throwing gasoline on an already lit fire! Skilled empathetic principals, on the other hand, recognize the signs and step in with strong emotional intelligence, often taking a few minutes each week to check in with team members and gauge how they are coping with teaching and life.

Second, principals must reveal sincere interest in the needs, hopes, and goals of faculty and staff. A harmonious campus climate and culture involves principals working collaboratively with team members always identifying the unique needs of individuals and then matching duty responsibilities to contribute to both professional performance and personal satisfaction.

Third, principals must be willing to assist all members of the learning community with professional as well as personal problems. The lines between work at school and life at home are thin and often increasingly blurred. Teachers are dynamic employees who shoulder and surmount problems on a daily basis; yet they somehow manage to maintain professional decorum and instructional responsibilities.

Support by and from the campus principal is an absolute and requires the leader to ensure open lines of communication are always in place and transparency is the word of the day—every day! Principals who foster psychological security and aid faculty in feeling comfortable to freely speak up and out and share in confidence are, in fact, empathetic leaders!

Fourth, principals must ensure the school is a family whereby all stakeholders are treated in a most empathetic manner. This means teachers are treated as professionals, instruction is data-driven, students are first and foremost in every consideration, parents are welcomed, positive principal and teacher energy is obvious, teamwork is contagious, teachers are developed into leaders, and strong principal leadership is not only visible, but also collaborative, facilitative, and distributed.

Fifth, principals must exhibit compassion when faculty or staff disclose a personal concern, issue, problem, or loss. Leader-to-follower connections matter. Empathetic leadership is a skill that principals must utilize to establish not only relationships but long-lasting bonds with those they are privileged to lead.

Concerns worthy of principal empathy and compassion relative to faculty or staff can come in the manner of life difficulties, including personal problems heightened by home-life considerations ranging from difficult parenting issues, childcare concerns, and husband-and-wife separation to divorce. The list, sadly, goes on and on.

Principal empathy also entails recognizing how loss can interfere with, if not damage, faculty or staff life. Losses usually come in the form of a death of someone close, someone loved and beloved such as a parent, spouse, child, or significant other, or an extended family member, or a friend. Loss can also be related to a spouse's job and income, home eviction, and natural, yet unexpected, disasters. Empathy in leadership is a quality exemplified by the age-old yet still so relevant Theodore Roosevelt quote: "Nobody cares how much you know, until they know how much you care" (BrainyQuote, 2021b).

Remember, walking in another person's shoes isn't about the walk or the shoes. It's all about being able to think as they think, feel what they feel, and understand why they are who they are, and where they've come from to where they are now. That's empathy! Essentially, empathy is the art of imaginatively placing your feet into the shoes of another, understanding their perspective on life, and using such to guide your own actions in relation to that individual as well as others.

CONCLUDING COMMENTS

Principals must employ seven key strategies to advance inclusive equity-based, equality-centered, empathy-focused, SEL, and well-being leadership and schooling. These strategies are 1) establish a vision and plan to improve student outcomes and accelerate teaching, leading, and learning; 2) cultivate coherent collaboration by providing consistent programs, policies, procedures, and resources; 3) promote and provide meaningful systems of support, evaluation, mentoring, and coaching; 4) develop initiatives to address achievement gaps for historically marginalized students; 5) meaningfully engage and involve learning community stakeholders (students, teachers, parents, families, and communities) by means of thoughtful planning and continuous improvement efforts; 6) establish cycles of inquiry and improvement and implement effective instructional practices for inclusive teaching, leading, and learning; and 7) empathetically coach for efficient, effective, and essential instructional services to improve the achievement of all learners, particularly those most at risk of failure and of being marginalized as learners.

FINAL THOUGHTS

Exceptional principals understand that empathy is a required skill for successful school leadership, and these leaders further recognize that empathy is not sympathy. Exceptional principals utilize four critical attributes of empathy: 1) take perspective, 2) remain nonjudgmental, 3) recognize an individual's emotional quotient, and 4) communicate a genuine understanding of an individual's emotional state.

Exceptional principals implement the seven elements of empathetic leadership by 1) displaying emotional intelligence; 2) possessing a mindset, a connection with an individual's needs; 3) being present and attentive to an individual's feelings; 4) paying attention by showing genuine interest and encouragement; 5) responding carefully and respectfully; 6) encouraging and supporting individuals in comments, actions, and behaviors; and 7) eliciting feelings, that is, bringing out the feelings of others and, furthermore, responding appropriately to the individual's feelings.

Exceptional principals utilize differing types of empathy such as awareness empathy, silent empathy, reflective empathy, and verbal empathy. By incorporating situational empathy, principals are able to reveal encouragement, understanding, and a listening ear. Yet, principals must be aware of the common barriers to empathetic leadership, which include fear, belittling attitudes, comparative comments, poor listening habits, judgment, finger-pointing, and a hard choice of words.

Exceptional principals incorporate seven empathetic habits by 1) focusing on the individual; 2) ensuring individuals can freely share their feelings; 3) avoiding offering opinions; 4) ensuring individuals feel empowered and supported; 5) imagining, understanding, and respecting what others are facing and dealing with in career and life; 6) reflecting upon, understanding the reasons for, and responding to the issues of others; and 7) recalling not only the Golden Rule but the Platinum Rule: *Treat others the way they want, and need, to be treated.*

Exceptional principals build a climate and culture of empathy by being observant of teacher burnout; showcasing a sincere interest in the needs, hopes, and goals of faculty; being receptive in assisting all members of the learning community; and exhibiting compassion when faculty disclose a personal concern, issue, problem, or loss.

Exceptional principals know that empathy is the art of imaginatively placing their feet into the shoes of others, understanding their perspective on life, and using such to guide their own actions in relation to others. These principals live by the axiom that "nobody cares how much you know until they know how much you care!"

DISCUSSION QUESTIONS

1. Consider the brief exchange between a principal and a little neighborhood boy:

    The principal, at home during a brief summer interlude, had several puppies she wished to sell. She placed a sign advertising the six pups at the edge of her yard nearest the street. As she was finishing driving the sign into the ground, she felt a tug on her short set. She looked down and gazed into the eyes of a little boy she suspected soon to be in one of the kindergarten classes at the school she led. The child said, "I want to buy one of your puppies."

    "Well," said the principal, "my puppies come from fine parents and cost a good deal of money." The boy reached into his pocket and pulled out a handful of coins and held the change up to the principal. The principal counted a quarter and two pennies. The little boy then said, "Is that enough?"

"Maybe so," replied the principal as she led the youngster into the open garage, where the mother and her puppies were resting. Inside the garage, the mother cautiously guarded her puppies and with a watchful eye followed the hands of the principal as she lifted each of the puppies out of their secure box. Five little balls of fur slowly attempted to walk. The little boy's eyes danced with excitement. As the dogs made their way around the small garage area, the little boy noticed something else stirring just inside the box.

Slowly, the principal lifted one last little puppy out, this one noticeably smaller than the rest. In a most awkward, stumbling manner, the littlest pup began hobbling toward the others, doing its best to catch up. Excitedly, the little boy pointed toward the runt of the litter and shouted, "I want that one!" The principal knelt down beside the boy's side and said, "Young man, you don't want that puppy. He will never be able to run and play with you like any one of these other pups."

With that the little boy stepped back from the principal, reached down, and began pulling up one leg of his scuffed-up jeans. It was then that he revealed a steel brace running down both sides of his leg attaching itself to a specially made shoe. Looking at the principal, the little boy said, "You see, miss, I don't run too well myself, and I know that my puppy will need someone who understands." With tears in her eyes, the principal reached down, picked up the little pup, handed it to the boy, and said, "No charge."

Sometimes, we learn best from example; in this case, reading from an account exemplifying empathy at work. Consider the questions which follow:

- Which of the seven elements of empathy are exhibited by the principal in the story? Was the principal's reaction to the boy pulling up his scuffed-up jeans empathy or sympathy? Explain.
- Which type of empathy was displayed by the principal in this particular story?
- Of the seven habits of highly empathetic principals, as noted within the chapter, which one best describes the principal as she relates to the little boy interested in purchasing a puppy.

CASE STUDY APPLICATION: THE EMPATHETIC PRINCIPAL: BUILDING UP PEOPLE IS AT THE HEART OF SCHOOL LEADERSHIP

Hazel Burke, principal at Marshall Road School, continued down the campus hallway making her way to the next classroom for another morning walk-through. She soon opened the door and entered George Baxter's reading class, where students were engaged in lively conversations about a book they had just finished reading. A poster session, with students rotating from station to station as part of a galley walk, was occurring and it was obvious to Principal Burke that Mr. Baxter's students were seriously engaged in the lesson objectives.

Soon after the arrival of Principal Burke, Mr. Baxter asked the students to take a "learning time-out" and explain to the school principal what was occurring in the day's lesson. Millie Ballard quickly raised her hand. Mr. Baxter called upon Millie and the young student took charge, leading an impromptu information account. Millie explained the following:

"See, Ms. Burke," Millie related to the principal, "we just finished reading a book called *Brady*, written by Jean Fritz and set in rural Washington County in southern Pennsylvania during the pre–Civil War era. Mr. Baxter told us it was a 'coming-of-age' story about a boy, Brady Minton. I loved this book because it's about an important part of history that everyone should understand. Mr. Baxter calls that 'having empathy'; right, Mr. Baxter?"

Another student, Deidre Thompson, then blurted out, "This book is about Brady, who is in the middle of a controversy between his mother, who is for slavery, and his father, who is against. Excitedly, Deidre stated, "Nearby his home, Brady finds an underground railroad. Ms. Burke, you know not a real railroad, you see, a bunch of top-secret trails, paths, and hush-hush roadways leading to safe houses that were used by slaves trying to escape to the north or to Canada."

Mr. Baxter then chimed, in noting that the students were involved in a learning activity that was more than a book report and the standard title of the book, author of the book, time and location of the story, and descriptions of the characters. "No, the students are leading this particular lesson and have come up with their own learning objectives and lesson activities to include character analyses, plot summaries, story themes, and differing cultural perspectives." Pointing toward one of the students, Mr. Baxter stated, "Even Harriet Johnson arranged for Mr. Harvey Griffin, an attorney with Butterworth, Hatch, and Noell who specializes in preventing discriminatory practices here in town, to speak to us about equity, equality, and empathy."

At the conclusion of the lesson, Principal Hazel Burke departed and returned to her office. Sitting behind her desk, she reflected upon the learning session and considered what she had observed, thinking about the term *empathy* and contemplating a campus personnel situation.

Pandora Spocks, social studies teacher at Marshall Road School, was regularly a thorn in Principal Hazel Burke's side. As the principal thought of the teacher antagonist, the school's assistant principal, Dr. Hubert Bombay walked in and said, "A penny for your thoughts?" Principal Burke looked up, smiled, and replied, "Well, in all honesty, I'm considering how to respond to Pandora Spocks. I just don't know what to make of her. She troubles me."

The assistant principal stared at his principal and then replied, "I'll tell you what to make of her. She's self-absorbed, always thinking of her own issues, and placing her needs above all others. I can describe her in four words: uncaring, judgmental, selfish, and insecure. Now, how's that for helping you to decide what to think of her?" Principal Burke shook her head and said, "No, Hubert, let's remain positive and focus on a more empathetic solution to working with Pandora."

Pandora Spocks was, by most estimates, all that Dr. Bombay had intimated. Another teacher, David Whale, described her as "hard to handle." Her numerous run-ins with other teachers, let alone Principal Burke, were common. Hazel Burke, as the campus leader, realized that she must be everything to Pandora Spocks that the social studies teacher was not to others. The principal thought to herself, "I know that Pandora is troubled, but it's so difficult being empathetic to such an individual."

APPLICATION QUESTIONS

1. What measure(s) must Principal Hazel Burke undertake in becoming more empathetic toward the teacher Pandora Spocks?
2. Which of the seven elements of empathy should Principal Burke employ when inviting Pandora Spocks in for a private office conversation? Explain your reasoning.
3. Identify which of the types of empathy could best aid Principal Burke in better understanding Pandora Spocks. Clarify how, by what means?
4. Identify which of the common barriers to empathetic leadership are displayed by Assistant Principal Hubert Bombay. How might Dr. Bombay overcome the identified barrier(s)?
5. Examine the chapter section entitled "Seven Habits of Highly Empathetic Principals" and identify which three of the seven habits would be most

beneficial for Principal Hazel Burke to incorporate when working with the social studies teacher, Pandora Spocks. Elucidate relative to your reasoning.

Chapter 7

Principal Action #7

Strengthen Your Own Personal Leadership Skills with the Social and Emotional Learning Instrument (A Principal Protocol)

"Without proper self-evaluation failure is inevitable!"—John Wooden, "The Wizard of Westwood," UCLA basketball coach, 1948–1975 (FancyQuotes.com, 2021)

DIRECTIONS

This inventory will take less than 10 minutes to complete. Examine each of the 25 statements and enter a score which best describes you as a principal of SEL. Respond to each statement accurately and honestly. Scoring interpretations will follow the statements presented.

Noted below are the scoring categories with numerical rankings. Place the identified numerical ranking in the blank prior to each statement based upon your own change perceptions.

1 (Never)   2 (Seldom)   3 (Sometimes)   4 (Often)   5 (Always)

As a principal or prospective principal:

_____ I ensure students have opportunities to share their opinions, serve in leadership roles, and engage in decision-making and problem-solving aspects of curriculum and instruction.

_____ I ensure faculty interact collaboratively in the development of instructional programs, routines, and procedures.

_____ I have regular positive and encouraging interactions with students in common areas and demonstrate a knowledge of students from a personal perspective.

_____ I interact with faculty and staff developing friendly, respectful, and collaborative relationships.

_____ I encourage students to genuinely care for each other by developing a sense of inclusivity among all students.

_____ I ensure faculty are engaged in regular professional development learning opportunities which cultivate SEL strategies for both students and adults.

_____ I lead faculty in utilizing highly effective restorative, instructive, and developmentally appropriate behavioral policies and actions.

_____ I support SEL language, practices, and priorities which are embedded in planning, implementation, and evaluation of curriculum and instruction.

_____ I agree that all faculty and staff, including the leadership team members, affirm students' diverse identities, culture, and home language during interactions, in instructional materials, and as part of curricular revision and development.

_____ I support teachers effectively incorporating instructional strategies and techniques which develop trusting relationships between students and faculty, and which are highly responsive to student needs.

_____ I regularly challenge teachers to incorporate learning activities which permit students to cultivate a sense of interdependence and inclusivity and, thus, I practice student-oriented social and emotional competencies.

_____ I lead faculty in promoting and permitting time for student self-regulation through verbal and non-verbal expected behaviors, thus reinforcing desired behavior rather than incorporating punitive punishments.

_____ I support and initiate consistent and predictable on-campus routines and procedures which contribute to a sense of safety and security all the while promoting SEL.

_____ I regularly ensure and provide for classroom time for coordinated culturally responsive instruction to foster social and emotional skills development.

_____ I communicate with teachers and verify their engagement relative to permitting students to lead instructional routines and/or learning activities—all followed with a high level of data fidelity.

_____ I communicate with teachers and foster high levels of student self-efficacy and learning relative to learning ownership.

_____ I expect, monitor, and verify that instructional settings are characterized by high expectations for learning for all students.

_____ I ensure SEL standards and competencies are clearly embedded within the academic day.

_____ I believe, expect, and verify that students regularly lead classroom discussions by which they formulate questions to critically, yet respectfully, challenge each other's thinking and learning.

_____ I ensure students co-construct and lead instructionally oriented classroom activities, always giving voice to student leadership roles and responsibilities in developing and engaging in learning activities.

_____ I lead regular and meaningful opportunities for families to be engaged in school-wide decision-making, permitting their sharing of ideas and providing essential feedback.

_____ I ensure families are treated with respect and are trusted, and I collaboratively interact with faculty and leadership.

_____ I lead with empathy and promote high levels of equity and equality.

_____ I establish roles, responsibilities, and timelines for the collection and dissemination of data to improve all aspects of SEL instruction.

_____ I incorporate collaboration as a means of change management.

SCORING INTERPRETATIONS

Calculate your total score and then correlate your score with the scoring comments below.

25–50 SEL is not a strong point in your skill development or leadership abilities or agenda. You have difficulty initiating or believing in this instructional approach to student learning and achievement. You tend to overlook focusing on immediate planning needs. Regrettably, you are most apt to fail to embrace the benefits and potential instructional aspects of SEL.

51–75 You understand a need for continued instructional improvement yet recognize you are held back for a variety of reasons from incorporating

SEL at your school. Concentrate on developing, in small segments, those SEL skills that will permit you to successfully lead a team of teachers to improve teaching and learning. Begin by collaborating with teachers and administrative team members to initiate the SEL process. Start with a small initiative or pilot program that will better ensure SEL implementation success. Then, continue to expand SEL instructional opportunities. Also, carefully read or reread each chapter in this text.

76–100 You are a skilled agent of not only mastering SEL skills but implementing this instructional enhancement at the campus level. However, remember that such a change is a never-ending process. Utilize professional development opportunities to expand SEL development efforts. Keep refining your personal SEL skills, maintaining an open-minded approach regarding opportunities to improve the school's curricular program, as well as teacher instruction and student learning.

101–125 You possess a keen understanding as to what makes SEL successful and why SEL is a critical aspect of teaching, leading, and learning as well as equity, equality, and empathy. You reveal a strong SEL knowledge base and possess a competent ability to manage, plan, and implement on-campus SEL. You are also a leader who will help teachers and parents overcome the challenges often associated with SEL as an instructional enhancement.

FINAL THOUGHTS

Be a school leader who brings all members of the learning community together to create a much stronger instructional program, a more positive learning and working culture, and a better organization led by a conviction that the well-being of all stakeholders is strongly correlated to the positive effects of SEL. Always lead with the strongest of moral and ethical values and conduct. Lead with a clear understanding of the value and importance of student equity and equality in all matters of education, society, and life. Lead with empathy and always help others reach a higher level of personal and professional well-being. Be an initiator of Principal Action #7: Strengthen Your Own Personal Leadership Skills with the Social and Emotional Learning Instrument (A Principal Protocol).

"Caring for the mind is as important and crucial as caring for the body. In fact, one cannot be healthy without the other."—Sid Garza-Hillman (*Approaching the Natural: A Health Manifesto*, 2013)

Note

CHAPTER 5

1. Recognize that the fictitious Walt Whitman School's six-point process to building racial equity is based in part on the Education Week article *6 Ways District Leaders Can Build Racial Equity*, written by Christina A. Samuels (June 18, 2020), which also reflects the teamwork of school systems and educators in Austin, Texas; Omaha, Nebraska; Akron, Ohio; Oklahoma City, Oklahoma; Jefferson County, Kentucky; and Ithaca, New York.

References

Ackerman, C. E. (2020). *25 fun mindfulness activities for children and teens.* Retrieved July 22, 2020, from https://positivepsychology.com/mindfulness-for-children-kids-activities/

Advancement Project. (2021). *George Floyd: One year later.* Retrieved October 3, 2021, from https://advancementproject.org/george-floyd-one-year-later/

AEI-Brookings Working Group on Poverty and Opportunity. (2015). *Opportunity, responsibility, and security: A consensus plan for reducing poverty and restoring the American dream.* Washington, DC: American Enterprise Institute for Public Policy and the Brookings Institution.

Agathangelou, F. (2015). *How volunteer activities build self-esteem.* Retrieved July 22, 2020, from https://www.healthyplace.com/blogs/buildingselfesteem/2015/09/volunteering-to-build-self-esteem

Atwell, M. N., & Bridgeland, J. (2019). *Ready to lead—2019.* Retrieved November 5, 2020, from https://casel.org/wp-content/uploads/2019/10/Ready-to-Lead_FINAL.pdf

AZ Quotes. (2021a). *Jesse Jackson quotes.* Retrieved December 15, 2021, from https://www.azquotes.com/quote/1425618

AZ Quotes. (2021b). *Malcolm X quotes.* Retrieved December 15, 2021, from https://www.azquotes.com/quote/865232

Banks, A. M., & Banks, J. A. (2021). *Civic education in the age of mass migration: Implications for theory and practice.* New York, NY: Teachers College Press.

Bastable, E., Fairbanks-Falcon, S., Nese, R., Meng, P., & McIntosh, K. (2019). *Enhancing school-wide positive behavioral interventions and supports tier 1 core practices to improve disciplinary equity.* Retrieved December 15, 2021, from https://files.eric.ed.gov/fulltext/ED603530.pdf

Beachboard, K. (2020). *Focusing on student well-being in times of crisis.* Retrieved August 14, 2020, from https://www.edutopia.org/article/focusing-student-well-being-times-crisis

Belfield, C., Bowden, A. B., Klapp, A., Levin, H., Shand, R., & Zander, S. (2015). *The economic value of social and emotional learning.* Published online by Cambridge University Press. Retrieved September 19, 2021, from https://www.cambridge.org/core/journals/journal-of-benefit-cost-analysis/article/div-classtitlethe-economic

-value-of-social-and-emotional-learningdiv/D9A12352A7CF1B39E9A2B7EA4C68F150

BrainyQuote. (2020). *Benjamin Franklin quotes*. Retrieved September 18, 2020, from https://www.brainyquote.com/quotes/benjamin_franklin_387287

BrainyQuote. (2021a). *Henry David Thoreau quotes*. Retrieved December 15, 2021, from https://www.brainyquote.com/quotes/henry_david_thoreau_386485

BrainyQuote. (2021b). *Theodore Roosevelt quotes*. Retrieved December 15, 2021, from https://www.brainyquote.com/quotes/theodore_roosevelt_140484

Brown Department of Education. (2021). *Addressing inequality in the classroom*. Retrieved December 7, 2021, from https://education.brown.edu/academics/graduate/master-arts-teaching/addressing-inequality-classroom

Budiman, A. (2020). *Key findings about U.S. immigrants for the Pew Research Center*. Retrieved October 1, 2021, from https://www.pewresearch.org/fact-tank/2020/08/20/key-findings-about-u-s-immigrants/

Cash, J. R. (1997). *Ralph Emery: On the Record* television interview. Retrieved October 16, 2021, from https://www.youtube.com/watch?v=WxXUEeFWRuk

Centers for Disease Control and Prevention. (2019). *Hispanic/Latino Americans and type 2 diabetes*. Retrieved July 24, 2020, from https://www.cdc.gov/diabetes/library/features/hispanic-diabetes.html

Chavez, N. (2021). *Confusion reigns in Texas as new law aims to restrict how race and history are taught in schools*. Retrieved October 16, 2021, from https://www.cnn.com/2021/09/01/us/texas-critical-race-theory-social-studies-law/index.html

Cherry, K. (2020). *How people's prejudices develop*. Retrieved October 1, 2021, from https://www.verywellmind.com/what-is-prejudice-2795476

Civic Enterprises and Hart Associates. (2013). *The missing piece: A report for CASEL*. Retrieved August 8, 2020, from https://casel.org/wp-content/uploads/2016/01/the-missing-piece.pdf

Civic Enterprises and Hart Associates. (2017). *Ready to lead: A national principal survey on how social and emotional learning can prepare children and transform schools*. Retrieved August 8, 2020, from https://www.casel.org/wp-content/uploads/2017/11/ReadyToLead_FINAL.pdf

Clark, A. (2020). *Social-emotional learning: What you need to know*. Retrieved August 9, 2020, from https://www.understood.org/en/learning-thinking-differences/treatments-approaches/educational-strategies/social-emotional-learning-what-you-need-to-know

Collaborative for Academic, Social, and Emotional Learning. (2011). *2015 CASEL guide: Effective social and emotional learning programs—Middle and high school edition*. Chicago, IL: Author.

Collaborative for Academic, Social, and Emotional Learning. (2020). *SEL impact*. Retrieved August 12, 2020, from https://casel.org/impact/

Counseling Teacher. (2021). *5 Benefits of social emotional learning*. Retrieved September 18, 2021, from https://thecounselingteacher.com/2020/02/5-major-benefits-of-social-emotional-learning.html

Darling-Hammond, L. (2018). *Kerner at 50: Educational equity still a dream deferred*. Retrieved August 6, 2020, from https://learningpolicyinstitute.org/blog/

kerner-50-educational-equity-still-dream-deferred?gclid=EAIaIQobChMI2MuSvP
GG6wIVA9bACh2sigJiEAAYASAAEgKNN_D_BwE

DeMatthews, D. E. (2018). *Community engaged leadership for social justice*. New York, NY: Routledge.

DeMatthews, D. E. (2019, January 4). Tap rainy day fund to aid Texas schools. *El Paso Times*. Retrieved July 28, 2020, from https://www.elpasotimes.com/story/opinion/2019/01/04/tap-rainy-day-fund-help-schools-david-dematthews-david-s-knight/2481604002/?from=new-cookie

DeMatthews, D. E., & Clarida, K. (2021). Opinion: Black school leaders need support as tensions threaten recruitment. *Austin American Statesman* (October 3). Retrieved October 4, 2021, from https://www.statesman.com/story/opinion/columns/your-voice/2021/10/03/black-school-leaders-need-support-tensions-threaten-recruitment/5937686001/

DePaoli, J. L., Atwell, M. N., & Bridgeland, J. (2017). *Ready to lead—2017*. Retrieved November 5, 2020, from https://www.casel.org/wp-content/uploads/2017/11/ReadyToLead_ES_FINAL.pdf

Dorn, E., Hancock, B., Sarakatsannis, J., & Viruleg, E. (2021). *COVID-19 and learning loss—disparities grow, and students need help: A McKinsey & Company report*. Retrieved September 18, 2021, from https://www.mckinsey.com/industries/public-and-social-sector/our-insights/covid-19-and-learning-loss-disparities-grow-and-students-need-help

Dowling, K., & Barry, M. M. (2020). Evaluating the implementation quality of a social and emotional learning program: A mixed methods approach. *International Journal of Environmental Research and Public Health, 17*, 3249.//**Give chapter pages**//

Dubow, E. F., & Rubinlicht, M. (2011). Coping. In B. B. Brown & M. Prinstein (eds.), *Encyclopedia of adolescence*. San Diego, CA: Academic Press.

Duckworth, K., Duncan, G. J., Kokko, K., Lyyra, A., Metzger, M., & Simonton, S. (2012). *The relative importance of adolescent skills and behaviors for adult earnings: A cross-national study*. Department of Quantitative Social Science, Working Paper 12-03. //**Give department location**//

Durlak, J. A., Weissberg, R. P., Dymnicki, A. B., Taylor, R. D., & Schellinger, K. B. (2011). The impact of enhancing students' social and emotional learning: A meta-analysis of school-based universal interventions. *Child Development, 82*, 405–432.

Einhorn, E. (2022). *The pandemic is affecting student behavior, prompting questions over discipline*. Retrieved January 3, 2022, from https://www.msn.com/en-us/news/us/the-pandemic-is-affecting-student-behavior-prompting-questions-over-discipline/ar-AASmhBl?li=BBnb7Kz

Espelage, D., Low, S., Polanin, J., & Brown, E. (2013). The impact of a middle school program to reduce aggression, victimization, and sexual violence. *Journal of Adolescent Health, 53*, 180–186.

European Commission against Racism and Intolerance (ECRI). (2021). *Combating racism and discrimination in and through education*. Retrieved October 2, 2021, from https://rm.coe.int/ecri-general-policy-recommendation-no-10-key-topics-combating-racism-a/16808b75f7

FancyQuotes.com. (2021). *John Wooden quotes*. Retrieved December 15, 2021, from https://quotefancy.com/quote/845172/John-Wooden-Without-proper-self-evaluation-failure-is-inevitable

Frey, N., Fisher, D., & Smith, D. (2019). *All learning is social and emotional: Helping students develop essential skills for the classroom and beyond*. Alexandria, VA: Association for Supervision and Curriculum Development.

Frost, R. (1923/1969). "Stopping by Woods on a Snowy Evening" from *The Poetry of Robert Frost*, edited by Edward Connery Lathem. New York, NY: Henry Holt and Company, Inc.

FutureEd. (2020). *How school suspensions affect student achievement*. Retrieved October 13, 2020, from https://www.future-ed.org/how-school-suspensions-affect-student-achievement/

Garza-Hillman, S. (2013). *Approaching the natural: A health manifesto*. Petaluma, CA: Roundtree Press.

Gentry, W. A., Weber, T. J., & Sadri, G. (2016). *Empathy in the workplace: A tool for effective leadership*. Retrieved December 15, 2021, from file:///C:/Users/R%20Sorenson/Downloads/EmpathyInTheWorkplace.pdf

Glossary of Education Reform. (2016). *Equity*. Retrieved August 6, 2020, from https://www.edglossary.org/equity/#:~:text=In%20education%2C%20the%20term%20equity%20refers%20to%20the%20principle%20of%20fairness.&text=It%20is%20has%20been%20said,%2C%20allocated%2C%20or%20distributed%20equally

Gonzales, D., & Wiener, R. (2017). *Our schools have an equity problem: What should we do about it?* Retrieved December 15, 2021, from https://www.edweek.org/policy-politics/opinion-our-schools-have-an-equity-problem-what-should-we-do-about-it/2017/05

Good Docs. (2020). *Personal statement*. Retrieved July 21, 2020, from https://gooddocs.net/products/personal-statement?utm_campaign=THE%20UNAFRAID&utm_medium=email&_hsmi=91684446&_hsenc=p2ANqtz-8-Q-OYrJwZ1piDMV7jCTdJtLRlHTQ5n6VEFF8FUsVUJf0vLK_hEK3oMdeFC-h_lZBXkJQ2uVJV41wNjSuRhzS3Yv6aBQ&utm_content=91459812&utm_source=hs_email

Goodreads, Inc. (2022). *Aristotle quotes*. Retrieved January 7, 2022, from https://www.goodreads.com/quotes/95080-educating-the-mind-without-educating-the-heart-is-no-education

Gopin, M. (1997). Religion, violence, and conflict resolution. *Peace & Change 22*(1), 1–31.

Govorova, E., Benitez, I., & Muniz, J. (2020). *How schools affect student well-being: A cross-cultural approach in 35 countries*. Retrieved July 22, 2020, from https://www.ncbi.nlm.nih.gov/pmc/articles/PMC7109313/

Gresham, F. M., MacMillan, D. L., & Bocian, K. (1996). Behavioral earthquakes: Low-frequency salient behavioral events that differentiate students at risk of behavior disorders. *Behavioral Disorders, 21*(4), 277–292.

Gupta, S., & Jawanda, M. K. (2020). The impacts of COVID-19 on children. *Acta Paediatrica, 109*(11), 15–48.

Hamilton, L. S., & Doss, C. J. (2020). *Supports for social and emotional learning in schools: Findings from the Rand Corporation American Teacher Panel.* Retrieved October 23, 2020, from https://www.rand.org/pubs/research_briefs/RBA397-1.html

Harvard Health Publishing. (2011). *Music and health.* Retrieved July 21, 2020, from https://www.health.harvard.edu/staying-healthy/music-and-health

Heng, T. (2018). *Coping strategies of undergraduates in response to academic challenges.* Retrieved August 25, 2020, from https://www.tcrecord.org/Content.asp?ContentID=21989

Howard, T. C. (2018). *We are failing our most vulnerable children.* Retrieved October 1, 2021, from https://www.edweek.org/leadership/opinion-we-are-failing-our-most-vulnerable-children/2018/06

Hunt, A. (2019). *How singing affects your brain—Six reasons to sing.* Retrieved July 24, 2020, from https://spinditty.com/learning/What-Singing-Does-To-Your-Brain

Jackson, C. K., Easton, J. Q., Kiguel, S., Porter, S. C., & Blanchard, A. (2020). *Linking social-emotional learning to long-term success.* Retrieved October 29, 2020, from https://www.educationnext.org/linking-social-emotional-learning-long-term-success-student-survey-responses-effects-high-school/

Jaitely, S. (2020). *7 habits of highly empathetic people.* Retrieved December 15, 2021, from https://empathyspark.com/7-habits-of-highly-empathetic-people/

Jones, B. L. (2020). *Reducing racism in schools: The promise of anti-racist policies.* Retrieved October 2, 2021, from https://education.uconn.edu/2020/09/22/reducing-racism-in-schools-the-promise-of-anti-racist-policies/

Jones, S. M., Brush, K., Bailey, R., Brion-Meisels, G., McIntyre, J., Kahn, J., . . . Stickle, L. (2017). *Navigating SEL from the inside out.* Cambridge, MA: Harvard Graduate School of Education with funding from The Wallace Foundation.

Jones, S. M., Brush, K. E., Ramirez, T., Mao, Z. X., Marenus, M., Wettje, S., . . . Bailey, R. (2021). *Navigating SEL from the inside out.* Cambridge, MA: Harvard Graduate School of Education with funding from The Wallace Foundation.

Jones, S. M., & Kahn, J. (2017). *The evidence base for how we learn: Support students' social, emotional, and academic development. Consensus statements of evidence from the Council of Distinguished Scientists.* Retrieved July 22, 2020, from https://eric.ed.gov/?id=ED577039

Kaufman, J. H., & Culbertson, S. (2021). *Addressing immigration doesn't end at the border—Schools need help.* Retrieved November 9, 2021, from https://staging.taktikz.com/addressing-immigration-doesnt-end-at-the-border-schools-need-help/

Kendziora, K., & Yoder, N. (2016). *When districts support and integrate social and emotional learning: Findings from an ongoing evaluation of districtwide implementation of SEL.* Retrieved July 22, 2020, from https://eric.ed.gov/?id=ED571840

Khandwala, A. J. (2020). *7 barriers to empathy that block effective leadership.* Retrieved December 15, 2021, from http://yellowspark.in/blog/7-barriers-to-empathy-that-block-effective-leadership/

Killough, A. (2021). *Texas book controversy: School administrator told teachers to include Holocaust books with 'opposing' views when explaining new state law.* Retrieved October 16, 2021, from https://www.msn.com/en-us/news/us/texas-book

-controversy-school-administrator-told-teachers-to-include-holocaust-books-with-opposing-views-when-explaining-new-state-law/ar-AAPyhvR?li=BBnb7Kz

KIND (Kids in Need of Defense). (2021). *Assisting unaccompanied children on both sides of the U.S.-Mexico border*. Retrieved October 3, 2021, from https://supportkind.org/wp-content/uploads/2020/10/KIND-Mexico-Fact-Sheet-Oct-2020_English.pdf

Kisling, J. (2021). *The difference between empathy and sympathy*. Retrieved December 15, 2021, from https://www.psychmc.com/articles/empathy-vs-sympathy

Korbey, H. (2021). *Teaching civics' soft skills: How do civics education and social-emotional learning overlap?* Retrieved October 27, 2021, from https://www.kqed.org/mindshift/58660/teaching-civics-soft-skills-how-do-civics-education-and-social-emotional-learning-overlap

Landau, M. D. (2021). *To overcome unconscious bias, you must recognize that it's deeply ingrained in your brain*. Retrieved October 1, 2021, from https://www.prevention.com/life/a35380041/unconscious-bias/

Las Americas Immigrant Advocacy Center. (2021). *General immigration relief*. Retrieved October 3, 2021, from https://las-americas.org/en/general-immigration-relief-program

LePage, B., & Jordan, P. W. (2021). *How are states spending their COVID education relief funds?* Retrieved October 16, 2021, from https://www.the74million.org/article/how-are-states-spending-their-covid-education-relief-funds/

Lewis, T. J., Mitchell, B. S., Horner, R. H., & Sugai, G. (2017). Engaging families through school-wide positive behavior support: Building partnerships across multi-tiered systems of support. In M. D. Weist, S. A. Garbzcz, K. L. Lane, & D. Kinkaid (Eds.), *Aligning and integrating family engagement in positive behavioral interventions and supports: Concepts and strategies for families and schools in key contexts* (pp. 31–42). Eugene, OR: OSEP Center for Positive Behavioral Interventions and Supports. Retrieved August 8, 2020, from http://www.pbis.org/Common/Cms/files/pbisresources/Family%20Engagement%20in%20PBIS.pdf

Linlin, L., Flynn, K. S., DeRosier, M. E., Weiser, G., & Austin-King, K. (2021). *Social-emotional learning amidst COVID-19 school closures: Positive findings from an efficacy study of Adventures Aboard the S.S. GRIN Program*. Retrieved September 18, 2021, from https://www.frontiersin.org/articles/10.3389/feduc.2021.683142/full

Mahoney, J. L., Durlak, J. A., & Weissberg, R. P. (2018). *An update on social and emotional learning outcome research*. Retrieved June 17, 2020, from https://kappanonline.org/social-emotional-learning-outcome-research-mahoney-durlak-weissberg/

Mayo Clinic. (2018). *Mindfulness exercises*. Retrieved July 28, 2020, from https://www.mayoclinic.org/healthy-lifestyle/consumer-health/in-depth/mindfulness-exercises/art-20046356

McIntosh, K., Simonsen, B., Horner, R., Swain-Bradway, J., George, H., & Lewis, T. (2020). *Getting back to school after disruptions: Resources for making your school year safer, more predictable, and more positive*. Retrieved August 8,

2020, from https://assets-global.website-files.com/5d3725188825e071f1670246/5e6bf89e521250ff6911564d_Back%20to%20School%20after%20Disruptions.pdf

Mediate Your Life. (2015). *Elements of empathy*. Retrieved October 16, 2021, from https://www.mediateyourlife.com/wp-content/uploads/2015/09/ElementsofEmpathy_Handout9-9-15.pdf

Montague, M., Enders, C., Cavendish, W., & Castro, M. (2011). Academic and behavioral trajectories for at-risk adolescents in urban schools. *Behavioral Disorders*, *36*(2), 141–156.

Moore, J. (2018). *Stressed out: Two-thirds of DC principals say they may leave job within 5 years, survey finds*. Retrieved September 21, 2020, from https://wtop.com/dc/2018/09/stressed-out-two-thirds-of-dc-principals-say-they-may-leave-job-within-5-years-survey-finds/#:~:text=More%20than%20than%20half%20of,in%20a%20similar%20national%20survey

Mungal, A. S., & Sorenson, R. D. (2020). *Steps to success: What successful principals do every day*. Lanham, MD: Rowman & Littlefield.

Napolitano, J. (2021). *RAND Corp says 321,000 undocumented children entered U.S. schools from 2016-2019, sparking need for more teachers, training, and funding*. Retrieved October 16, 2021, from https://www.the74million.org/article/rand-corp-says-321000-undocumented-children-entered-u-s-schools-from-2016-2019-sparking-need-for-more-teachers-training-and-funding/

National Association for the Advancement of Colored People. (2021). *Leading the fight for justice, equity, and equality*. Retrieved October 3, 2021, from https://naacp.org/

Nachin, L., & Sorenson, R. D. (2021). *Coordinated leading: Principals and counselors—Vision, expectations, support, scheduling, and resource allocations*. Unpublished manuscript, Department of Educational Leadership and Foundations, The University of Texas at El Paso, El Paso, TX.

National Center for Education Statistics. (2021). *Racial/ethnic enrollment in public schools*. Retrieved October 1, 2021, from https://nces.ed.gov/programs/coe/indicator/cge

Noble, T., McGrath, H., Wyatt, T., Carbines, R., & Robb, L. (2008). *Scoping study into approaches to student wellbeing. Report to the Department of Education, Employment and Workplace Relations*. Brisbane, Australia: Australian Catholic University.

NotableQuotes. (2022). *Mahatma Gandhi quotes*. Retrieved January 7, 2022, from http://www.notable-quotes.com/g/gandhi_mahatma.html

Office for Civil Rights. (2021). *Education in a pandemic: The disparate impacts of COVID-19 on American students*. Retrieved September 18, 2021, from https://www2.ed.gov/about/offices/list/ocr/docs/20210608-impacts-of-covid19.pdf

Olson, L., & Toch, T. (2021). *Changing the narrative: The push for new equity measures in education*. Retrieved January 3, 2022, from https://www.future-ed.org/wp-content/uploads/2021/11/FUTUREED_REPORT_EQUITY.pdf

Options for Youth. (2021). *Four major benefits of social/emotional learning*. Retrieved September 18, 2021, from https://ofy.org/blog/four-major-benefits-of-socialemotional-learning/

Organisation for Economic Co-operation and Development. (2021). *Social and emotional skills: Well-being, connectedness, and success.* Retrieved August 25, 2021, from https://www.oecd.org/education/school/UPDATED%20Social%20and%20Emotional%20Skills%20-%20Well-being,%20connectedness%20and%20success.pdf%20(website).pdf

Osterman, K., & Kottkamp, R. (2004). *Reflective practice for educators: Professional development to improve student learning.* Thousand Oaks, CA: Corwin.

PoemHunter.com. (2022). *How do I love thee.* Retrieved January 8, 2022, from https://www.poemhunter.com/poem/how-do-i-love-thee/

Princeton-Brookings. (2017). *The future of children.* Retrieved December 15, 2021, from https://www.wallacefoundation.org/knowledge-center/Documents/FOC-Spring-Vol27-No1-Compiled-Future-of-Children-spring-2017.pdf

Psychology Today. (2019). *Mindfulness.* Retrieved July 22, 2020, from https://www.psychologytoday.com/us/basics/mindfulness

Quotefancy.com. (2021). *Barack Obama quotes.* Retrieved December 15, 2021, from https://quotefancy.com/quote/771229/Barack-Obama-Learning-to-stand-in-somebody-else-s-shoes-to-see-through-their-eyes-that-s

QuotePark.com. (2021). *Confucius quotes.* Retrieved January 7, 2022, from https://quotepark.com/quotes/750206-confucius-to-see-what-is-right-and-not-do-it-is-the-worst-co/

Raman, L. (2012). *7 elements of empathy.* Retrieved December 15, 2021, from http://lalitaraman.com/2012/04/22/7-elements-of-empathy

Ramirez, M. (2021). *White people in the US have long controlled public institutions: Racial progress has paid the price.* Retrieved October 3, 2021, from https://www.msn.com/en-us/news/us/white-people-in-the-us-have-long-controlled-public-institutions-racial-progress-has-paid-the-price/ar-AAP6m5S

Richard, P. (2021). *The 4 attributes of empathy.* Retrieved December 15, 2021, from https://cpamoncton.ca/en/ressources/blog/251-the-4-attributes-of-empathy

Robbins, S. P., & Judge, T. A. (2019) *Organizational behavior: Concepts, controversies, and applications.* New York, NY: Pearson Education, Inc.

Robinson-Kiss, S. (2020). *I'm a Black therapist, and this is why neglecting your mental health could be lethal today.* Retrieved July 24, 2020, from https://www.nbcnews.com/know-your-value/feature/i-m-black-therapist-why-neglecting-your-mental-health-could-ncna1231253

Saad, L. (2020). *Roundup of Gallup polling coverage.* Retrieved September 27, 2020, from https://news.gallup.com/opinion/gallup/308126/roundup-gallup-covid-coverage.aspx

Samuels, C. A. (2020). *6 ways district leaders can build racial equity.* Retrieved October 2, 2020, from https://www.edweek.org/ew/articles/2020/06/18/6-ways-district-leaders-can-build-racial.html

Schwartz, H. L., Hamilton, L. S., Faxon-Mills, S., Gomez, C. J., Huguet, A., Jaycox, ... Wrabel, S. L. (2020). *Early lessons from schools and out-of-school time programs implementing social and emotional learning.* Retrieved October 20, 2020, from https://www.rand.org/pubs/research_reports/RRA379-1.html

Shelton, N. N. (2021). *Shelton: Black and Brown school leaders are essential for real educational equity, but they need support in order to succeed*. Retrieved October 16, 2021, from Shelton: Black and Brown School Leaders Are Essential for Real Educational Equity, but They Need Support in Order to Succeed | The 74 (the74million.org)

Sklad, M., Diekstra, R., DeRitter, M., Ben, J., & Gravestein, C. (2012). Effectiveness of school-based universal social, emotional, and behavioral programs: Do they enhance students' development in the area of skill, behavior, and adjustment? *Psychology in the Schools, 49*, 892–910.

Smiley, A. (2020). *Why school wellness isn't just for kids: Many teachers are stressed and depressed*. Retrieved September 21, 2020, from https://ohsonline.com/articles/2020/02/07/why-school-wellness-isnt-just-for-kids-many-teachers-are-stressed-and-depressed.aspx#:~:text=Another%202017%20study%20from%20University,stress%20levels%2C%20depression%20and%20anxiety

Sorenson, R. D. (2020a). *Our family values are none of your business: Voices from the field of practice—Parents respond to SEL*. Unpublished interviews, Department of Educational Leadership and Foundations, The University of Texas at El Paso, El Paso, TX.

Sorenson, R. D. (2020b). *Time, fear, initiative, or ignorance: Why principals are to blame?* Unpublished interviews, Department of Educational Leadership and Foundations, The University of Texas at El Paso, El Paso, TX.

Sorenson, R. D. (2022). *The 8-point school leadership compass*. Unpublished manuscript, Department of Educational Leadership and Foundations, The University of Texas at El Paso, El Paso, TX.

Sorenson, R. D., & Goldsmith, L. M. (2009). *The principal's guide to managing school personnel*. Thousand Oaks, CA: Corwin.

Sorenson, R. D., & Goldsmith, L. M. (2018). *The principal's guide to school budgeting*. Thousand Oaks, CA: Corwin.

Steinberg, M. P., & Lacoe, J. (2017). What do we know about school discipline reform? Assessing the alternatives to suspensions and expulsions. *Education Next, 17*(1), 44–52.

Superville, D. R. (2020). *Principals need help building anti-racist schools*. Retrieved October 2, 2021, from https://education.uconn.edu/2020/09/22/reducing-racism-in-schools-the-promise-of-anti-racist-policies/

Superville, D. R. (2021). *Principals need social-emotional support, too*. Retrieved December 15, 2021, from https://www.edweek.org/leadership/principals-need-social-emotional-support-too/2021/09

UNESCO. (2021). *Distance learning solutions*. Retrieved January 21, 2021, from https://en.unesco.org/covid19/educationresponse/solutions

U. S. Commission on Civil Rights. (n.d.). *Racial and ethnic tensions in American communities: Poverty, inequality, and discrimination*. Retrieved October 1, 2021, from https://www.usccr.gov/files/pubs/msdelta/ch3.htm

Victoria State Government Education and Training. (2021). *Promote mental health: Social and emotional learning*. Retrieved September 18, 2021, from https://www.

education.vic.gov.au/school/teachers/health/mentalhealth/Pages/socialemotion.aspx

Wallace Foundation. (2021). *Navigating SEL from the inside out: Looking inside and across 33 leading SEL programs—A practical resource for schools and OST providers*. Retrieved December 15, 2021, from https://www.wallacefoundation.org/knowledge-center/Documents/navigating-social-and-emotional-learning-from-the-inside-out-2ed.pdf

Wilding, M. (2019). *7 habits of highly empathetic people: Follow these steps to focus on what matters—connection*. Retrieved December 15, 2021, from https://www.inc.com/melody-wilding/7-habits-of-highly-empathetic-people.html

World Book Dictionary. (2019). *Definition of terms*. Chicago, IL: Author.

York-Barr, J., Sommers, W., Ghere, G., & Monthie, J. (2005). *Reflective practice to improve schools: An action guide for educators*. Thousand Oaks, CA: Corwin.

Young Minds. (2019). *Six ways you can boost your self-esteem*. Retrieved July 22, 2020, from https://youngminds.org.uk/blog/six-ways-you-can-boost-your-self-esteem/

Zimmer-Gembeck, M. J., & Skinner, E. A. (2016). The development of coping: Implications for psychopathology and resilience. In D. Cicchetti (Ed.), *Developmental psychopathology: Risk, resilience, and intervention* (pp. 485–545). John Wiley & Sons, Inc. Retrieved July 24, 2020, from https://doi.org/10.1002/9781119125556.devpsy410

Index

academic achievement, 61
accountability friends, 7
Ackerman, C. E., 11
active learning and teaching, 30
activism, 12; student, 27
activities, SEL, 42, *43*, *44*
AEI. *See* American Enterprise Institute for Public Policy
afterschool learning sessions, 4
Alabama, voting rights in, 74
Allen, Josh, 91
American Enterprise Institute (AEI) for Public Policy, 55
The American Rescue Plan, 38
Aristotle, 35
Armitage, Willi, 49
assessments, 23
asylum-seeking students, 85
attendance, school, 4–5
attention, paying, 96
awareness: identity, 56; self-awareness, *43*, *44*; social, *43*, *44*, 45
awareness empathy, 97

Ballard, Millie, 106
barriers: to empathetic leadership, 99; to equality and equity, 79
Bastable, E., 58
Baxter, George, 106

Beachboard, K., 50, 51
Benitez, I., 22
bias, 82–84
Black Americans, voting rights of, 74
Black Lives Matter, 1
Black students, 79
Bombay, Hubert, 107
Briggs, Dana, 49
Brookings Institution, 55
Browning, Elizabeth Barrett, 73
Budiman, A., 84
Burke, Hazel, 106–7
burnout, teacher, 101

campus counselors, 20
The Carpenters, 12
Carter, Cinnamon, 48–49
CASEL. *See* Collaborative for Academic, Social, and Emotional Learning
case studies: on empathy, 106–7; on equity and equality, 91–93; on gun violence, 32–33; on SEL, 48–52, 69–70; on well-being, 16–17
Cash, Johnny, 80
The Center on Positive Behavioral Interventions and Supports, 58
Changing the Narrative (Olson and Toch), 81

126   *Index*

Cherry, K., 83
Civic Enterprises, 37
civics education, 46
clarity, of expectations, 41
class meetings, *43*
climate: of empathy, 101–3; positive, 9; school climate measures, 38
code-switching, 58
Collaborative for Academic, Social, and Emotional Learning (CASEL), 55
collective actions, 82
Collier, Barney, 49
communication, 50–51
Community Engaged Leadership for Social Justice (DeMatthews), 81
compassion, 102
confidence, 36
Confucius, 89
consistency, 51
control, 51
coping strategies, 9–14; laughter, 13–14; mindfulness, 11; modeling positive coping behaviors, 12; music, 12; positive self-talk, 11–12; self-esteem, 10; service, 14; sharing, 11; singing, 12–13; staying engaged and connected, 12
counselors, 20
COVID-19, 1, 25–26, 88
COVID Relief Aid for Education, 38
critical thinking, 60–61
cultural responsiveness, 56–60
culture: of empathy, 101–3; norms, 41; open, 9; of well-being, 21–26
curriculum, well-being in, 26–29

daily greetings, *43*
Dalhgren-Frost, Marcie, 6
data analysis and evaluations, expanded, 62–63
Davis, Anissa, 69–70
debate, 27
decision-making: data-based, 62; responsible, *43, 44*
DeMatthews, David, 81

Diaz, Zulma, 70
disciplinary issues, 4–5
discrimination, 82–84
dispositions, of students, 27
disruption, 26, 65
district initiatives, 39
district support, 23
Dixon, Pete, 91
Dorn, E., 64
Doss, C. J., 36
"do we really matter?" (case study), 16–17
drop-out rates, for immigrant students, 85
Durlak, J. A., 55
Dymnicki, A. B., 55

Elementary and Secondary Education Act (1965), 78
elementary school, SEL activity examples in, *43*
emotional intelligence, 96
emotional learning. *See* social and emotional learning
empathy, 21; barriers to, 99; case study for, 106–7; climate and culture of, 101–3; conclusion to, 103; as critical tool, 97–100; defined, 95–96; elements of, 96; final thoughts on, 103–4; habits for, 100–101; as norm, 101–3; signs of, 98; social justice and, 81–86; sympathy versus, 96; types of, 97–98
emptying, of "stinking-thinking" emotions, 7
enforcement, of expectations, 42
engagement, 12; hope and, 8
enthusiasm, 9
equity and equality, 21, 59–60; case study on, 91–93; comparative examples of, 77–78; data for, 63; defined, 76–77; equity versus equality, 73–74; final thoughts on, 89–90; for immigrant students, 84–85; importance of, 78–81;

meaning of, 75–81; principal leadership and, 74–75; racism in schools and, 87–89; social justice and, 81–86
European Commission against Racism and Intolerance, 87
Every Student Succeeds Act (2015), 78
expectations, for SEL, 41–42
expulsions, 4–5

facts, hard, 2
Fairbanks-Falcon, S., 58
fear, SEL and, 38
feeling, eliciting, 96
fidelity data, 62–63
fiscal/community lifeline, 24
Floyd, George, 1
Franklin, Benjamin, 19
Frasier (TV series), 11
free therapy, 7
FutureEd, 81
"F-word," 58–59

Gallup survey (2020), 8
Gandhi, Mahatma, 89
Garver, Catherine, 69–70
George, H., 49
Ghere, G., 45
goals, 23
Golden Rule, 101, 104
Goldsmith, L. M., 22, 55, 99
Good Docs, 20
Govorova, E., 22
Griffin, Harvey, 106
gun violence, 32–33
Gupta, S., 25

Hamilton, L. S., 36
Hancock, B., 64
hard facts, 2
Hart Associates, 37
Heng, T., 14
Hispanic students, 78–79
hope, 8–9
hopelessness, 8

Horner, R., 49
Horner, R. H., 49
Howard, T. C., 87

identity awareness, 56
immigrant students, 84–85
improved student behaviors, 61
improvement, 20
initiative, SEL and, 38
injustices, social, 74
institutional racism, 87
instructional programs, 28
interactive modeling, 30

Jawanda, M. K., 25
Johnson, Alice, 91
Jones, B. L., 87
journal writing, *43*
justice. *See* social justice

Kaufman, Seymour, 91
Keith, Bill, 70
Khandwala, Aparna Joshi, 99
Kobolowski, Chanice, 5–6
Kottkamp, R., 45

Landau, M. D., 83
language skills, 30
The Las Americas Immigrant Advocacy Center, 85
Latinx students, 60
laughter, 13–14
leadership teams, 28
learning community leaders, 4
learning environment, 27
learning gaps, 64–65
learning support systems, 14
legislative bills, racism and, 87
Leos-Monsivais, Margarita, 32–33
Lewis, T., 49
Lewis, T. J., 49
life satisfaction, 2
logical consequences, 30
Loomis, Helen, 91

Maxwell, Halcyon, 16–17
Mayo Clinic, 11
McIntosh, K., 49, 58
McIntyre, Liz, 91
McKinsey & Company, 64
Meng, P., 58
mindfulness, 11
mindset, possessing, 96
Mitchell, B. S., 49
modeling, interactive, 30
Monthie, J., 45
Mungal, A. S., 50, 83
Muniz, J., 22
music, 12

Nachin, L., 96
National Center for Children in Poverty, 84
negative impact indicators, 25
negativity, 14
Nese, R., 58
non-compliance, 60
norms: culture, 41; empathy as, 101–3

Obama, Barack, 95
objectives, 23
O'Casey, Francis Aloysius, 32–33
OECD. *See* Organization for Economic Co-operation and Development
Olson, Lynn, 81
Open Circle (program), 36
open culture, 9
optimism, 8–9
Organization for Economic Co-operation and Development (OECD), 84, 86
Osterman, K., 45

pandemic, COVID-19, 1, 25–26, 88
parents, SEL as important to, 39–40
Parker, Alma, 16–17
pedagogy, 27
pessimism, 8
Pew Research Center, 84
Phelps, Jim, 48–49

Platinum Rule, 101, 104
positive climate, 9
positive coping behaviors, modeling, 12
positive psychology, 2
positive self-talk, 11–12
prejudice, 82–84
present, being, 96
Princeton-Brookings, 55
principals of color, 78–79
problem-solving, reflective, 45
programmatic success, 24
psychology, positive, 2
public education: equity and equality in, 78; for immigrant students, 85
"push-in" classroom instruction, 4

queries, student, 28

racism, 87–89
Raman, L., 96
Ramos, Sua, 86
Rand Corporation, 36–37, 85
read a-louds, *43*
reflective empathy, 97
reflective problem-solving, 45
relationship-building, *43*
relationship development, 45
Responding to Resisters, 65
responsible decision-making, *43, 44*
Responsive Classroom (program), 36
responsive curriculum, 27–29
responsive instruction, 29, *30*
Robinson-Kiss, Sheila, 1, 15
Roosevelt, Theodore, 102
routines, for SEL, 41
RULER (recognizing, understanding, labeling, expressing, and regulating emotions), 36

Sarakatsannis, J., 64
Schellinger, K. B., 55
school climate measures, 38
school counselors, 20
secondary school, SEL activity examples in, *44*

SEL. *See* social and emotional learning
self-awareness, *43, 44*
self-care, 1
self-esteem, 10
self-maintenance, 45
self-management, *43, 44*
self-reflection, 60–61
self-reliance, 14
self-talk, positive, 11–12
service, 14
sharing, 11
Shelton, N. N., 79
silent empathy, 97
Simonsen, B., 49
singing, 12–13
situational appropriateness, 57–58
small group interaction, 30
social and emotional learning (SEL): academic achievement and, 61; activities, 42, *43, 44*; appreciation of, 36–37; benefits of, 55–65; case studies on, 48–52, 69–70; challenges with implementing, 65–67; critical thinking and, 60–61; cultural responsiveness and, 56–60; defined and explained, 35–40; essential attributes for, 42–45, *43–44*; expanded data analysis and evaluations, 62–63; expectations for, 41–42; final thoughts on, 47, 67–68; implementation of, 40–42; importance to principals, 36–39; importance to teachers, students, and parents, 39–40; improved student behaviors and, 61; instrument, 109–12; learning gaps and, 64–65; routines for, 41; solution of, 37–38; struggle of, 37; team involvement and, 63–64; well-being and, 45–46
social awareness, *43, 44*, 45
social injustices, 74
social interaction, 12
social justice: bias, prejudice, and discrimination and, 82–84; defined, 81–82; for vulnerable students, 84–86
social management, 45
Sommers, W., 45
soothing music, 12
Sorenson, R. D., 22, 50, 83, 96, 99
Spocks, Pandora, 107
state accountability standards, 39
"stinking-thinking" emotions, 7
student activism, 27
student behaviors, improved, 61
student queries, 28
students of color: equity and equality for, 75, 80, 81; immigrant students, 84–85; Latinx, 60; principals of color and, 78–79; in public schools, 78; racism and, 87–89; well-being for, 4, 5
student success teams, 4
Sugai, G., 49
Superville, D. R., 14, 87
supportive environment, 57
surveys, 25
suspensions, school, 4–5
Swain-Bradway, J., 49
sympathy, empathy versus, 96

Taylor, R. D., 55
teacher burnout, 101
teacher preparation programs, 39
team involvement, 63–64
technological/learning support systems, 14
therapy, free, 7
Thompson, Deirdre, 106
Thoreau, Henry David, 89, 95
time, SEL and, 37, 38, 66–67
Toch, Thomas, 81
training, consistency in, 24
Tremaine, Neva, 16–17

uncertainty, 26, 65
understanding, lack of, for SEL, 38
UNESCO, 25

values-based education/learning, 27
verbal empathy, 98
Viruleg, E., 64
voice, 56–57
voting rights, of Black Americans, 74
vulnerable students, social justice for, 84–86

Wallace Foundation, 55
Weissberg, R. P., 55
well-being, 1–2; case study on, 16–17; conclusion, 14–15; considerations for, 6–7; coping strategies for, 9–14; critical examination of, 2–3; culture of, 21–26; in curriculum, 26–29; disciplinary issues and, 4–5; hope and, 8–9; learning and, 3; modeling and promoting, 5–7; of personnel, 5–6; problem associated with, 3–4; program, *23–24*; promoting practice of, 20–26; SEL and, 45–46; "what are you doing, now?" for, 19–20
well-being committee, 23
well-being plan, 24
wellness, 1–2. *See also* well-being
Whale, David, 107
"what are you doing, now?," 19–20
Whitaker, Joey, 69–70
Wooden, John, 109
working harder, 14

X, Malcolm, 81

York-Barr, J., 45
YouTube Therapy, 7

About the Author

Dr. Richard Sorenson, professor emeritus, resides in Cypress (northwest Houston), Texas. He is the former director of the Principal Preparation Program and chairperson of the Educational Leadership and Foundations Department at The University of Texas at El Paso (UTEP). Dr. Sorenson earned his doctorate from Texas A&M University at Corpus Christi. He served for 25 years as a social studies teacher, assistant principal, principal, and associate superintendent for human resources.

Dr. Sorenson has worked with graduate students at UTEP in the areas of school-based budgeting, personnel, educational law, and leadership development. He was previously named UTEP's College of Education Professor of the Year.

Dr. Sorenson is an active writer with numerous professional journal publications. He has authored nine principal leadership textbooks, as well as teacher resource guides and student workbooks. He has been actively involved in numerous professional organizations, including the Texas Elementary Principals and Supervisors Association and the Texas Association of Secondary School Principals, for which he has conducted annual new-principal academy seminars.

Dr. Sorenson has been married to his best friend, Donna, for the past 46 years and they have two adult children, Lisa (son-in-law, Sam) and Ryan (daughter-in-law, Nataly), and three young grandchildren, Savannah, Nehemiah, and Amelia—all of whom are the pride and joy of his life.

www.ingramcontent.com/pod-product-compliance
Lightning Source LLC
Chambersburg PA
CBHW032216230426
43672CB00011B/2572